Drawing Babar

DRAWING
Babar

EARLY DRAFTS
AND WATERCOLORS

Christine Nelson

WITH AN ESSAY BY
Adam Gopnik

FOREWORD BY
William M. Griswold

The Morgan Library & Museum, New York

Drawing Babar: Early Drafts and Watercolors is made possible by The Florence Gould Foundation.

Chilton Investment Company, Inc. is the corporate sponsor.

Generous support is also provided by The Grand Marnier Foundation, T. Kimball Brooker, The American Society of the French Legion of Honor, Inc., Hubert and Mireille Goldschmidt, and Barbara and James Runde.

We gratefully acknowledge the cooperation of the Consulate General of France in New York and the Cultural Services of the Embassy of France in New York.

LIBRARY OF CONGRESS CATALOGING-IN-PUBLICATION DATA
Nelson, Christine.
 Drawing Babar : early drafts and watercolors / Christine Nelson ; with an essay by Adam Gopnik ; foreword by William M. Griswold.
    p. cm.
  ISBN 978-0-87598-151-2 (alk. paper)
  1. Brunhoff, Jean de, 1899–1937—Characters—Babar. 2. Brunhoff, Laurent de, 1925—Characters–Babar. 3. Babar (Fictitious character) 4. Children's stories, French–Illustrations. 5. Elephants in literature. 6. Elephants in art. 7. Water-color painting, French. I. Gopnik, Adam. II. Title.
  PQ2603.R9453Z79 2008
  843'.912–dc22   2008024224

HARDCOVER ISBN: 978-0-87598-151-2
SOFTCOVER ISBN: 978-0-87598-152-9

COVER: Jean de Brunhoff, study for pp. 6–7 of *Histoire de Babar, le petit éléphant*

Printed in the United States of America

Contents

Director's Foreword

In March and April 1938, New Yorkers had the opportunity to view two brief but memorable exhibitions of French art held within a block of each other on Fifty-seventh Street (Figs. 1–2). As *Time* magazine reported, "Manhattanites last week repaired to the Pierre Matisse Gallery to see fifteen paintings by a 30-year-old Parisian known as Balthus." On the same page of the magazine, in the column next to its announcement of Balthus's American debut, *Time* described a very different exhibition held concurrently a few doors down at the New York galleries of Durlacher Brothers: sixty-six watercolors by "a pleasant Parisian gentleman named Jean de Brunhoff."* De Brunhoff's Babar stories were already well-known and well-loved in the United States, and his brother Michel, the Paris editor of *Vogue*, had arranged a memorial exhibition with a New York venue. The explosive career of the young Balthus was just beginning; that of Jean de Brunhoff—dead from tuberculosis at age thirty-seven just a few months before—had already ended.

Thanks to the efforts and vision of Charles E. Pierce, Jr., the Morgan's director from 1987 until his retirement at the end of last year, Balthus and de Brunhoff have come together again—twenty blocks south and seventy years later—at The Morgan Library & Museum. In 1997, at the midpoint of Charlie's tenure, the Pierre Matisse Foundation donated to the Morgan the complete record of the activities of the highly influential Pierre Matisse Gallery, including many letters from Balthus to Matisse and the checklist of that seminal 1938 installation. And in 2004, thanks in large part to Charlie's enthusiasm and persistence, the Morgan acquired the extraordinary Babar collection that is the subject of this catalogue. It includes preliminary drawings and manuscripts, as well as the watercolor and hand-lettered printer's dummy, for *Histoire de Babar, le petit éléphant* (1931), the first book in the series that went on to become one of the most successful in the history of children's literature. These materials were added to the collection thanks to the generosity of Jean de Brunhoff's three sons—Laurent, Mathieu, and Thierry—who made a partial gift of their father's work, and The Florence Gould Foundation, which donated funds to purchase the balance of the material. (Additional funding was drawn from the Morgan's Acquisitions, Fellows Endowment, Gordon N. Ray, and Heineman funds.) We also salute the de Brunhoff brothers for choosing to donate their father's drawings for *Le voyage de Babar* (1932) and *Les vacances de Zéphir* (1936), along with Laurent de Brunhoff's preliminary work

* *Time*, 4 April 1938, p. 45.

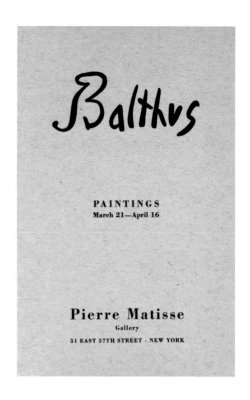

for *Le château de Babar* (1961), to the Bibliothèque nationale in Paris, thus paying tribute to Babar's French roots.

In addition to the *Histoire de Babar* collection, the Morgan also acquired in 2004 a large array of drawings for *Babar et ce coquin d'Arthur* (1946), the first book by Laurent de Brunhoff, who continued the Babar series after his father's death. This material was an outright gift from Laurent de Brunhoff, for which we at the Morgan are deeply grateful. Indeed, without his gracious benefaction and ongoing generosity, this exhibition and catalogue would not have been possible. Laurent's wife, Phyllis Rose, the writer and longtime professor of English at Wesleyan University, and Mary Ryan of the Mary Ryan Gallery, New York, have also provided extraordinary support to the Morgan as we have prepared to present our Babar collection to the public.

The Babar collection and the Pierre Matisse Gallery records were landmark additions to the Morgan's department of Literary and Historical Manuscripts made on the watch of my distinguished predecessor. While both acquisitions illustrate the Morgan's efforts to expand the chronological reach of its holdings into the twentieth century and beyond, they also reflect an approach to collecting consistent with that established by Pierpont Morgan and J. P. Morgan, Jr.: to build on existing strengths and add new materials that reflect the finest and most influential artistic achievements of an era.

The Babar collection joins an astonishing group of manuscripts and printed editions of highly important works spanning more than five centuries of European children's literature. Important early highlights include Lazare de Baif's *De re navali libellus*, printed in Paris in 1537 and considered by many to be the first book expressly illustrated for children; the earliest and only known copy of the first edition of *The History of Tom Thumbe* (London, 1621); and a unique copy (once owned by the great collector Charles Fairfax Murray) of *Les contenances de la table*, printed in Lyons in 1487, a French courtesy book to which the Babar series may be considered a modern heir.

The Morgan also holds a beautiful copy of the most enduring of all French children's stories: a 1695 presentation manuscript of the classic tales of Mother Goose (*Contes de ma mère l'oye*) by Charles Perrault, preceding the first printed edition by two years, with seven gouache illustrations for such stories as "Puss-in-Boots" and "Sleeping Beauty." Among holdings of more recent vintage are picture letters from Beatrix Potter to young Noël Moore, including one featuring the antics of her pet rabbit, Peter; a large collection of drawings and letters by the Victorian children's book illustrator Kate Greenaway; and the manuscript and illustrations for one of the most popular of all French stories—*Le petit prince*, written in New York by Antoine de Saint-Exupéry a decade after the publication of *Histoire de Babar*. All these manuscripts, printed editions, and drawings contribute to our understanding of the creation of these seminal works of art—a process that is explored in this catalogue by Christine Nelson, the Morgan's Drue Heinz Curator of Literary and Historical Manuscripts, who also organized the exhibition.

We are honored that Adam Gopnik, one of our country's most distinguished authors, has contributed an essay that reflects his deep engagement with French culture and his understanding of the power of storytelling. I am profoundly grateful to The Florence Gould Foundation, whose generous contributions have made possible the acquisition of the Babar collection as well as the publication of this catalogue and the presentation of the accompanying exhibition; to Chilton Investment Company, Inc., for corporate sponsorship; and The Grand Marnier Foundation, T. Kimball Brooker, The American Society of the French Legion of Honor, Inc., Hubert and Mireille Goldschmidt, and Barbara and James Runde for their generous support. Thanks are due to the Sherman Fairchild Foundation for funding the work of conservation fellow Denise Stockman. We are also especially appreciative of the cooperation of the Consulate General of France in New York and the Cultural Services of the Embassy of France in New York.

William M. Griswold, *Director*
The Morgan Library & Museum

Author's Acknowledgments

I am grateful above all to Laurent de Brunhoff for the humor and grace he brings to life and storytelling, for the beauty of the illustrated books he continues to create for readers throughout the world, and for his generosity in making his own work and that of his father available to the public in perpetuity at The Morgan Library & Museum. To Laurent's brothers, Mathieu and Thierry de Brunhoff, who joined him in making the extraordinary gift of their father's earliest Babar drawings and manuscripts to the Morgan, my colleagues and I give our deepest thanks. And to the late Jean and Cécile de Brunhoff, who created the elephant child who left the jungle to enrich our human world, thank you.

This catalogue and exhibition would not have been possible without the boundless generosity of Phyllis Rose and Mary Ryan, both of whom provided endless support, information, and access, clearly inspired by their deep love for Laurent and delight in his work. The Florence Gould Foundation provided essential financial support both for the acquisition of the *Histoire de Babar* collection and for the exhibition and catalogue. Mary and John Young were essential advocates of the project from the start. My thanks also go to Barbara Pierce, whose 1994 conversation with Laurent de Brunhoff set in motion the events that would lead to the Morgan's acquisition of the rich collection described in this catalogue, and to her husband, Charles E. Pierce, Jr., the Morgan's director from 1987 to the end of 2007, for his enlightened leadership and determination in bringing the Babar collection to the Morgan.

I am grateful to many colleagues and collaborators at the Morgan. Among them are Reba Snyder and Denise Stockman, who brought skill and sensitivity to the conservation treatment of every piece of paper in the Morgan's Babar collection; Marie Trope-Podell for guidance in matters of French culture and language; Declan Kiely, Robert Parks, and Bill Griswold for strong institutional support; Anna Lou Ashby for expertise in the field of children's literature; Leslie Fields for conducting the initial evaluation and description of the collection; Marilyn Palmeri and Eva Soos for managing the complex photographic aspects of this catalogue; Benjamin Bailes and Robert DeCandido for various forms of technical support; Karen Banks for bringing this book to fruition; and Patricia Emerson for her characteristically elegant editorial work. I also appreciate the assistance of John Alexander, Fran Barulich, John Bidwell, Isabelle Dervaux, Inge Dupont, Rhoda Eitel-Porter, Anita Masi, Rose Miesner, Maria Molestina, Blair Payne, Maggie Portis, Andrea Stillman, Kristina Stillman, and Roger Wieck.

Many people outside the Morgan have also been helpful in various ways: Jo Ellen Ackerman for her sensitive catalogue design; Schecter Lee and Rob Gullixson, who photographed nearly 300 pages of Babar manuscripts, drawings, and printed material; Andrea Immel, curator of the Cotsen Children's Library at Princeton University, for sharing her vast knowledge of children's literature and publishing; James Serpell of the University of Pennsylvania School of Veterinary Medicine and Nigel Rothfels of the University of Wisconsin-Milwaukee for insight into Western cultural interpretations of animals, particularly elephants; Christine Moisset and Frank Chance of the University of Pennsylvania for guidance in French and Japanese linguistic matters; Judith F. Dolkart of the Brooklyn Museum for information on James Tissot's work; Tabitha Hanslick-Nguyen of the Library at the Fashion Institute of Technology for assistance with French fashion periodicals; Francis Robinson of the University of London for his knowledge about the Mughal emperor Babur; and Nicholas Fox Weber and Anne Meinzen Hildebrand for their important published work on the art and literature of Jean and Laurent de Brunhoff. I am also grateful to Bruce Benjamin, Daniel Frank, Paul Holdengräber, and Ella Serpell.

Adam Gopnik, whose fertile mind never ceases to amaze me, brought a fresh perspective to our reading of a classic story, and his eight-year-old daughter, Olivia, offered insightful comments. Finally, thanks to my family, Ella Comberg and David Comberg, who inspire me—like Babar and Celeste after their marriage—to reflect on my great *bonheur*.

Christine Nelson
Drue Heinz Curator of Literary and Historical Manuscripts
The Morgan Library & Museum

Freeing the Elephants

Babar Between the Exotic
and the Domestic Imagination of France

ADAM GOPNIK

A chain of elephants, trunks and tails linked, wander, with a mix of real energy and complacent pride, against a red background down the endpapers of a children's book. Thus begins one of the stories that most delight the imagination of the modern child and his distant bookend, the modern adult—Jean de Brunhoff's *Babar*. The simple image evokes not just the organic made mechanical, according to Bergson's famous formula for comedy—wild animals regimented like soldiers—but the quite raw and the very cooked: instinct and organized display in harmony. The Babar books by de Brunhoff *père* and *fils* are among the half dozen picture books that seem to fix not just a character but a whole mood, a way of being, even a civilization, for early imprinting. An elephant, lost in the city, does not trumpet with rage but rides a department store elevator up and down, until gently discouraged by the storekeepers. A city, logical and lucid, Hausmann's paradise in the savannah, rises in the middle of the barbarian jungle. Once seen, Babar the elegant, yet homey, Frenchified elephant is not forgotten. Even after we have passed on, moved beyond to other, seemingly more complicated images, something of his style sticks stubbornly in our heads and imprints his civilization on our minds. It remains one of the few enterprises begun by a father that was continued by his son in more or less the same style. (J. W. Audubon's continuation of his father's *Quadrupeds* is the only other modern instance that comes to mind, but in that case the father was alive when the son began to carry on the work.) The Babar books have, with Bemelmans's *Madeline* and Sendak's *Where the Wild Things Are*, become part of the common language of childhood, the library of the early mind. There are few parents who haven't tried them and the rare small child who doesn't like, or even love them. If the power of hand-made imagery needs to be vindicated in an era of machine-processed visual product, that power lies here: kids stare at anything they are shown on screens and then the next thing after. Kids like to look at Babar, and they remember him later.

Of all the improbable books to have a controversial literature attached to them, the Babar books would seem the most improbable, but they do. This may be in part because current academic study of literature makes itself known *only* through controversy and argument—no one gets a PhD by saying, "Yummy!" By now a controversial literature is possible about *anything*: there will soon be an attack on *Goodnight Moon* for being authoritarian, and a case will be made insisting that the title character of *The Runaway Bunny* does have every right to be terrified of that omnipresent, inescapable Mrs. Portnoy of a mother. But the Babar controversy—*faut-il brûler Babar?* / "must we burn Babar?", as one inquisitor puts it in a famous French idiom—is different because, though overwrought, it isn't really trivial: it touches on questions that are, on their own, real enough and enduring.

The Babar books have been implanted in a surprisingly resilient and hydra-headed argument about the uses of imagery and the subtleties of imperialist propaganda. Babar, as not one but many impassioned interpreters have insisted, is a French allegory of colonization, as seen by the complacent colonizers: the naked African natives, represented by the "good" elephants, are brought to the imperial capital, acculturated, and then sent back on a civilizing mission to their homeland. They ape—or is it elephant?—their colonial masters, and those elephants that have been most successfully colonized dominate those that have not. The ordinary animals are made to feel shame for not imitating the manners of their colonial masters, while the animals that resist—the rhinoceri in this allegory—are exterminated. The trusty, Europeanized elephants are, like dictators in West Africa, then made trustees of the system, consuls for the colonial power. To be made French is to be made human and to be made superior. The straight lines and boulevards of Celesteville, the argument goes, are the sign of enslavement. The true condition of the animals—to be naked, on all fours, in the jungle—is made shameful to them, while to become an imitation human, dressed and upright, is to be given the right to rule. Through such subtle imprinting, such early propaganda, the argument concludes, are the premises of imperialism treated as natural, and an allegory of elephants becomes a narrative of permanent oppression.

Nor is this argument meant "tongue in cheek," to use that awful phrase, or unseriously: there really is a question about meaning and the uses of children's literature here. As a Babar-using, and Babar-loving, reader and parent, it's easy to sneer at this and, as is usual, to write it off as "politically correct." (Far more genuinely racist things have been enabled by sneering at their critics as "politically correct" than have ever been stopped by political correctness.) But the detractors touch on a real point: none of us has any difficulty seeing that, say, *Little Black Sambo*, for all his pancake-eating charms, needs to be thought through before being introduced to young readers, while a book, to take an extreme case, from 1930s Germany about the extermination of long-nosed rats by obviously Aryan cats would go on anyone's excluded list, however beautifully or charmingly drawn.

Yet the critics of Babar surely in the long run miss the matter, the real subject, of Babar. It seems to this reader at least that they, and we, have missed the point and missed it in ways that make us miss some of the larger uses of children's literature and art and to mistake a work of subtle satiric artistry for one of crude propaganda. The de Brunhoffs' Babar saga is not an unconscious instance of the French colonial imagination—it is a self-conscious comedy *about* the French colonial imagination and its close relation to the French domestic imagination. The point of the classic early books of the 1930s—*The Story of Babar* and *Babar the King,* particularly—and what delights us about them, is not that they are the vehicles of a subliminal or implicit plot, but that they make an explicit and intelligent point: the lure of the city, of civilization, of style and order and bourgeois living are real, for elephants as for humans. The costs of those things are real, too, in the perpetual care, the sobriety of effort, they demand. The happy effect that Babar has on us, and our imaginations, comes from this knowledge—from the child's strong sense that while it is a very good thing to be an elephant, still, the life of an elephant is dangerous, wild, and painful. It is therefore a safer thing to be an elephant in a house near a park. Fables for children work not by pointing a moral but by complicating the moral of a point. Dancing along the edge of this experience is what makes fables for children count. The child does not dutifully take in the lesson that salvation lies in civilization, but, in good Freudian terms, takes in the lesson that the pleasures of civilization come with discontent at its constraints: you ride the elevator, dress up in the green suit, and go to live in Celesteville, but an animal you remain—the dangerous humans and rhinoceri are there to remind you of *that*—and delight in being. This lesson—that escape from the constraints that button you up and hold you is good—stands. That the constraints and buttons can be alluring nonetheless speaks to the child's, and our own, experience of the world-as-it-is. We would all love to be free untrammeled elephants, but we all long for a green suit. It is not that Babar simply exemplifies our imagination of French civilization and of the French mission to civilize.

Instead, the elephant examines that imagination and with the delicacy and comic sensitivity one would expect from a creature with such a long and sensitive trunk.

All children's stories that "work" at all begin with a simple opposition of good and evil, of straightforward innocence and envious corruption. Any bedtime storyteller knows how quickly and how effectively this opposition works: a good young pitcher is met by an evil outfielder, and suddenly a terrifying moral universe of threat and revenge erupts in the semidarkened room to delight and terrify the child. It is startling to discover how well, and how fast, this kind of opposition works, and how crude it can be and still work. ("Stop, now!" the child will cry about an invention of evil, cardboard thin and scarcely more than a minute old.) While the good hero or heroine has to be particularized with flaws and idiosyncrasies or risk disappearing into the great sludge of goodness, the evil force is, oddly, the more powerful the less distinct he is. Voldemort is scary because he cannot be named; Sauron is as unimaginable to his creator as he is to his readers (and when he is imagined more thoroughly, in the accessory Tolkien sagas, he becomes a little dull, another bad guy in armor). Villainy is itself so interesting that the villain doesn't have to be interesting to serve as the alternative force.

In no children's literature is this creation of dull and faceless evil as effective, and propellant, as it is in the Babar saga. "Page two of *Babar*" is a code idiom among New York mothers (and the occasional New York father) for the entire issue of what is right to expose our children to. (Though it's actually the sixth numbered page in the book, and the fourth page in the story, it seems to get internalized as page two: i.e., the second element in the story after the introduction of the nursery elephant idyll.) It is there that Babar's mother, after rocking her little elephant to sleep, is murdered, with casual brutality, by a squat (and white) hunter. Those who do read the page to their children believe that a heightened sense of evil heightens the experience of the story; those who don't think that a murder as brutal and casual as that will haunt the child and increase her fears. (It is easy to scoff at these second, "overprotective" parents until one discovers that children are in fact upset for a long time by the wrong image. One eight-year-old I know could not sleep for years—truly years—because of an accidental exposure to Rackham's Rumplestiltskin, all bony fingers, dubious size, and long nose.) The pro–page-twoers think that without the incident, the story is robbed of all motive and pathos; the no–page-twoers think that it's just too hard, too early, and too brutal, so they turn the story into one of a little elephant who merely wanders into Paris—not in itself such a bad premise. Sendak, in his lovely appraisal of Babar, recalls thinking that the act of violence that sets Babar off was not suffi-

ciently analyzed—that it was left unhealed and
even untreated—and that some of Babar's excessive
appetite for normalcy is owed to this unhealed
trauma.[1] Nicholas Fox Weber, in his fine study of
the art of the elephant saga, suggests that the normalcy is exactly the cure: that his "apparent indiffer-
ence to his mother's shooting is a by-product of the
essential drive to see beauty and continue living no
matter how tragic the past."[2]

Fig. 1. Like the closing pages of *Histoire de Babar*, in which the newly married elephants reflect on their good fortune, Henri Rousseau's *Sleeping Gypsy* (1897) depicts the desert as an enchanted place.

Whatever the motive, amnesiac or therapeutic,
the moment when, in *Babar*, the lost and mother-
less elephant enters the French city—Paris, surely,
though backing up on the desert and also standing in for French colonial cap-
itals from Saigon to Casablanca—is one of the magical moments in children's
literature. What makes it magical is how subdued and simple the moment is,
creating a lovely, perpetually renewed tension between the savannah and the
city, around which the whole series will be structured. The exoticism of the
Babar story is, from the beginning, obviously a fifth-arrondissement exoticism,
like that of the douanier Rousseau, whose harmless but rapacious paintings of
wild animals, inspired by visits to the zoo, have much of the same sober
charm as Jean de Brunhoff's. (And the dream of the desert as an enchanted
place, which takes such a powerful form in Rousseau's matchless *Sleeping
Gypsy* [Fig. 1] as in de Brunhoff's unforgettable nocturne of Babar and his
bride, connects them both.)

But there is a deeper connection, made visible in the language of style,
between this kind of French made-at-home exoticism and the domestic
charm of Babar—between, if you like, the first Rousseau and the second
Rousseau, between Jean Jacques's idea of the native genius of children and
Henri's vision of the romantic appeal of North Africa. France during the 1930s
was in transition from the old unashamedly predatory model of imperialism to
one that insisted on the *mission civilisatrice*—the benevolent and unity-
making gathering of different races into one French commonwealth—and
simultaneously in transition from a model of work and labor as their own
reward to one in which the reward of irksome labor was French family leisure.
The likeness of *foyer* and the savannah was organic and part of the pattern of
the society, rather than a new or insidious thing in Babar.

This kind of double "primitivism" of the hearth and the heathen, the
foyer and the faraway, is charmingly apparent in the books' style, even more
than in the obvious and much-argued-over storyline. What initially strikes one
about Jean de Brunhoff's preliminary drawings is how much more conven-

tionally "masterly"—the work of an obviously accomplished draftsman—they are than the finished drawings. The sketches are sinuous and bending and authoritative as de Brunhoff searches out form and presentation. The "finish" of de Brunhoff's surviving, and quite conservative, oil paintings meant for adult collectors is one of the most obvious things about them.

The finished Babar drawings, by contrast, are famously and beautifully simple, real small masterpieces of the *faux-naïf*: the elephant faces reduced to a language of points and angles, each figure cozily encased in its black ink outline, long stretches of pure color backgrounding friezelike arrangements of figures. De Brunhoff's style is not at all "dumbed down," but it is deliberately simplified. One recognizes the style at once as a decorative, illustrator's extension of the manner of fauvist drawing of the previous quarter century, an illustrator's version of Matisse, Dufy, and Derain, which by the 1930s had already been filtered and defanged and made part of the system of French design.

Out of fear of appearing to equate big and small, critics find it necessary to use the word *defanged.* But it does not really apply. From its beginnings, high fauve style, in the hands of Matisse in particular, had a direct and authoritative relationship to children's art and the idea of childhood. Picasso saw this keenly and talked about it without fear (though possibly with a hint of condescension), speaking often of how crucially the drawings of Matisse's children had affected their father's art, and for the better, supplying a kind of domestic primitivism, an African art of the nursery.

One sees this clearly in the childlike primitivism of such prime Matisse as *The Painter's Family* (Fig. 2), with its Roz Chast figures and its boys in red playing chess—an image that belongs in the same form world as the Babar domestic scenes—or even in a masterpiece as sophisticated as the incomparable *Piano Lesson* of 1916 (Fig. 3) where the play between the oppressive weight of French teaching and the gasping attempt at pleasure weighs on the boy. (*The Piano Lesson* is a kind of internal image of the inner life of Arthur and Zephir when the Old Lady forces them to learn cello and violin in *Babar the King.*) The faux-naïf manner is part of the renewed simplification of art in early-twentieth-century France, and it can draw equally on the distant and exotic and on the near-at-hand and juvenile. The natural traffic, implicit in Babar, between the exotic elephant and the French nursery is already implied, in more complex form, in Matisse's *Moroccans* (1915–16; Fig. 4), in which the remote decorative style of French-colonized Africa is rephrased in terms of the metropolitan faux-naïf. A kind of basic stuff, an underlying common language of simple sublime form connects the Minoan, the African, and the Moroccan with the miniature citizens of the metropolis. The tightrope between the exotic and the domestic that the Babar books walk along is not

nursery art alone but central to the French imagination of the first half of the twentieth century—the great desert opens onto the great city; the beautiful patterning of the carpet gives life to the gray light of the Ile de France; we dream of the elephants, and the elephant dreams of a green suit and a motor-car. (It is, as the Marxists like to say, no accident that the children's dining room of the French ocean liner *Normandie* was decorated with de Brunhoff's elephants. It is sad for us that they are now lost; they were the good animal totems of French voyaging.)

This higher version of the "natural traffic" in form between the exotic and the avant-garde, exemplified by Matisse, has been criticized repeatedly in recent years as unnatural commerce: the cosmopolitan avant-garde exploits and steals from the abject colonized just as brutally as the cosmopolitan forces of capitalism steal from the "natives'" resources. Yet to accept some part of

Figs. 2–3. In his drawings for the domestic scenes in the Babar series, Jean de Brunhoff employed a simplified style that echoed the domestic primitivism of such works as Matisse's *Painter's Family* (1911; above left) and *The Piano Lesson* (1916; above right).

Fig. 4. The "natural traffic" between the exotic and the domestic, central to French art of the first half of the twentieth century, is evident in Matisse's *Moroccans* (1915–16; below).

this—Picasso's belief that he was in touch with Africa by looking at its appro-
priated masks is indeed a form of the imperialist imagination—is not to pretend that prophylactics can be placed between peoples. The traffic between
styles—high and low, exotic and childlike—between imaginary elephants and
French fashion illustrators is what gives art of all kinds its life and spice. All art
is mongrelized, subject to what the French call *metissage*. Not just in its overt
stories but in its deeper grammar and visual style, Babar is an instance of the
French imperial imagination at a happy moment in its history. But to say this
is merely to register a point. And it is to miss, in Matisse as much as in de
Brunhoff, the self-conscious wit and joy with which the traffic between exotic
and domestic runs.

◆   ◆   ◆

Seeing how deep and organic this traffic is, at a level of style and not just story,
may make us see the "politics" of Babar in a more complex way, too. Reading
about the Babar books in the controversial literature, it's easy to forget that
Babar is, first and last, meant to be funny, amusing, and that Babar is, from
beginning to end, an elephant who talks and walks, and children know it: the
story is happening to creatures that children know in advance do not have
thoughts, ride elevators, wear suits, or build buildings. This kind of displace-
ment of human thoughts and feelings into imaginary animals can lead to
point-by-point allegories (as in Orwell's paint-by-numbers *Animal Farm*) or to
something more subtle. With the Babar books, we are from the beginning not
in the world of animal allegory but of animal *fable*: not the kind of story in
which human conduct is dressed up in animal costume but the kind in which
part of the joke resides in the way the obvious animalness of the protagonist
makes the absurdity of the depicted human behavior apparent. Though
Aesop's stories are conventionally called fables, they have some of the didactic
quality we associate more often with allegory: the particular attributes of the
animal define a specific ruling passion—foxes represent greed, turtles, perse-
verance, and so on. In the animal fable properly (or idiosyncratically) so-called,
the underlying absurdity of all human social behavior is underlined once we
see an animal imitating it. An animal that attempts human ambitions—to
become an astronaut or conduct an orchestra—is inherently ridiculous and
makes the ambition ridiculous as he pursues it. That's why Daffy Duck is *daffy*;
he's seriously pursuing lives that look loopy once he pursues them.

Babar, similarly, is, first and always, an elephant that takes on the role of
the bourgeois patriarch (and monarch) and reveals that role's touching absurdity
even as the elephant assumes it. Celesteville is a *comic* creation, a dream city of
the animals. The point of the moment in *Babar the King*—the central book in

the Babar saga—when the rhinos and elephants are at war is not to show that the rhinos are evil. It is to show that war between nations in reality is as absurd as war among animals looks on the page. In the same way, by becoming French, the elephants reveal the absurd and contrived elements of the French national character. But they do it in a way that also reveals a sober good intention at the heart of that character, the civilizing intention. Celesteville is a dream city of French classical corporatism—but it is a parody city of the French corporatist dream, of what is still called "solidarity" in France. In fact, I cannot think of a better guide to what the French *mean* by "solidarity," and why it still has such a hold on the French imagination, than a reading of *Babar the King.* The corporatism of the economy of Celesteville is beautifully expressed in the drawing of the elephants at their various occupations (Fig. 5), as Cartesian and logical as a poster from the pedagogical instruments house Deyrolle:

_25_

> If Barbacol wants a statue for his mantelpiece, he asks Podular to carve one for
> him, and when Podular's coat is worn out Barbacol makes a new one to order for
> him. . . . Hatchibombotar cleans the streets, Olur repairs the automobiles, and,
> when they are all tired, Doulamor plays his cello to entertain them. . . . As for
> Coco, he keeps them all laughing and gay (p. 24).

Fig. 5. In *Babar the King,* Jean de Brunhoff depicted an ordered elephant society in which everyone has a useful occupation.

The great problem of any society, animal or human—what to do when Hatchibombotar doesn't *want* to clean the streets and thinks that some other elephant ought to do it instead, while he wears the crown—is left unaddressed. Note, too, that there are no bankers, or stockbrokers, in Celesteville. Capitalism is not rejected but elided, or eluded, as are unnecessary "middlemen," in this perfect Comtian economy in which each does his job and receives his goods. There is to be no ambition, either, no emphasis on the upwardly mobile individual elephant. That is an American elephant's notion.

This idea of a unified community—not Marxist and thoroughly "bourgeois" in its extreme evaluation of the professions over the proletariat— remains powerful in France. For the reward for this serene corporatism is apparent on the next page of *Babar the King*—it provides exceptional leisure: the elephants work in the morning and take off the entire afternoon. (The Babar saga begins, of course in the 1930s, just as the Popular Front and the five-week holiday are in motion in France, creating the actual leisure-principled society that persists to this day.) And then this society provides continuity with the classical traditions—the elephants all attend a production, bewigged and formal, of the Comédie-Française. Surely the happy effect this has on the reader, and the elephants, is not because we (or they) have been propagandized to accept colonial hegemony. This isn't a portrait at a distance of an imaginary colonial city. It is, instead, an affectionate parody, made close up, of a nascent if idealized French society. The fragility of this society—and its actual inability to resist the rhinoceri—only intensifies the pathos and affection we feel for its depiction.

The great institution of this transformation in the French vision of empire, and what it brings home, was the Colonial Exposition of 1931, held at about the same time that Jean de Brunhoff began the Babar books. The ideas of that exposition are part of the stories' emotional atmosphere. Their temple is the still hallucinatory central pavilion out in the thirteenth arrondissement. (For a long time it had an afterlife as the Musée national des Arts d'Afrique et d'Océanie and is now, with the transfer of its collections to the Musée du quai Branly, to be made into a museum of immigration—telling, ironically, the story of how the colonized changed France.) The point of its hypervivid outdoor polychrome murals, depicting the whole of the French empire, is that France radiates its sun outward and is rewarded with the returning reflection of the fringes, which bring everything from pineapples to sculpture back into the hexagonal orbit. (And, let it be said, this dream of reciprocal benevolence is not entirely notional: the global supremacy of French soccer over the past decade is entirely a result of the expansion of the French empire and its ability to collect newly made Frenchmen with new skills.)

It is not merely easy but necessary to criticize this record: yes, of course, the smiling face on the native is an enforced smile, concealing centuries of humiliation and exploitation. All that no one can doubt. But literature is not simply history allegorized. All stories take place in the imaginative, not the literal, world. For children, the imaginative leap that lets them see that the remote and threatening belong to the same pattern of life as the near-at-hand and domestic is simultaneously reassuring (They're like us!) and empowering (I can go elsewhere and not be lost! I'm like them!). Works of art, for children or grown-ups, are layered; we need not buy the whole of the ideology to buy a part of its effect. We read Kipling's *Kim* or *Jungle Book* not because we are accomplices to empire but because we recognize the energy that comes from the friction between two worlds. We love Babar because we recognize the dream palace of French civilization and know it both as a dream and a symbol of a civilization. The duality brings a smile to our lips.

◆　◆　◆

So a "certain idea of France," in de Gaulle's phrase, is at the heart of the appeal of the Babar books. What is that idea, and how does it differ from our idea of England or America? First, it is urban: it has to do with Paris. Next, it is *ordered*—its most familiar sign is symmetry, as in the urban planning of Celesteville. It is also hedonistic and has to do with pleasure. All children's books, of course, have something to do with disorder and order and their relation. In our century, different ideas of order have each been represented in children's literature by a city or a country. One could make it diagrammatic, in an Audenesque manner, in this way:

ENGLAND AND LONDON (in the Mary Poppins stories and *The Wind in the Willows* and, in a slightly different way, *The Hobbit*): order is internal, found at home, part of the natural world of the nursery and riverbank; disorder lies beyond, at times threatening but more often beckoning as a source of joy and Dionysian possibility. See the chapter entitled "The Piper at the Gates of Dawn" in *The Wind in the Willows* or the celestial circus in *Mary Poppins*. Order is comforting but plain; disorder is beautiful, both threatening and romantically alluring. We escape the nursery for the disorder of the park.

FRANCE AND PARIS (in the Babar and Madeline books; also in the film and book of *The Red Balloon*): disorder is internal, psychological; the natural world is accepted as inherently *coquin*, "mean," or potentially violent; order lies beyond and needs to be created by constant infusions of education and city planning; it is a source of Apollonian pleasure. Paris is the place where you go up and down in the elevator. Madeline's will is to walk along the parapet; Miss Clavell wakes every night to sense that something is not right. The girls walk in two straight lines to hold disorder at bay. When disorder arrives—Madeline and Pepito's time with the gypsies, Babar and Celeste's imprisonment in the circus—it is, if not pleasurable, than predictable, taking the form of routine. Disorder is the normal mess of life, what rhinos like. Order is what elephants (i.e.,

Frenchmen) achieve at a cost and with effort. To stray from built order is to confront the man with a gun.

AMERICA AND NEW YORK (in *From the Mixed-Up Files of Mrs. Basil E. Frankweiler, The House on East 88th Street, Stuart Little, The Pushcart War,* or *Harriet the Spy*): Neither order nor disorder is natural. The world normally oscillates unpredictably between them, producing battles and freaks. The best we can find are small secret islands of order. See the stalls and secret rooms in *The Mixed-Up Files,* the pushcart vendor's secret headquarters in *The Pushcart War.* Everything turns around the individual child and her ability to create a safe miniworld of her own.

Each of these repeated schemes has its allure, for our children and ourselves. We go to the imaginary France and Paris for sudden glimpses of evil—the boys breaking the balloon, Babar's mother dying—set off by satisfying visions of aesthetic bliss—the balloon rising above the city in chromatic harmony, the Celesteville Bureau of Industry situated near the Amusement Hall. We go to the imaginary London to satisfy our longing for adventure and the undefined elsewhere, which returns us safely in the end to Cherry Tree Lane. And we go to the imaginary New York for the pleasure of the self-made: to see two children actually hide and live in a museum; to see an alligator (or a mouse) absorbed uncontroversially into a normal life. And each of these schemes reflects a history—the French vision for children a natural consequence of a troubled nation with a violent history in search of peace; the English vision a natural consequence of a peaceful nation with a reformist history and a search for adventure; and the American one of a sporadically violent and individualistic country with a strong ethos of family isolation and improvised rules.

Reflecting realities, all these varieties of order, all these kinds of books, also reflect desires, dreams. That is why it is also no accident that the great children's books have often been made in exile from the cities of their subjects. The most "London" of the Mary Poppins books, *Mary Poppins in the Park,* was written by Pamela Travers on Fifty-fourth Street in Manhattan, where she had come with her adopted child to wait out the Second World War. The Madeline books were drawn in New York as well, and Saint-Exupéry's *Little Prince* on Long Island. Although Babar is at one level an exception, begun in the real French domestic idyll so touchingly evoked by Laurent de Brunhoff in his lovely memoir of his youth, it is also, in another way, an exile's book—a dream of the French empire made at a far remove. Although one might easily overdramatize, or sentimentalize, this distance, one feels it nonetheless. Nor is it insignificant that the dream image of the city and country arises just as the real place is in crisis and not long after in definitive trauma. *Babar,* like *Mary Poppins, Madeline,* and *The Little Prince,* is forged and keeps the manners of the 1930s and then the 1940s, when the beautiful bourgeois cities seemed likely to be destroyed, first by their own internal cruelties and then by the Lord of Slaughter from outside.

As Christine Nelson points out in her essay, there is a haunting resemblance between the climactic image of *Babar,* when the new king and his queen commune with the African stars in the desert, and that of *The Little Prince,* when the snake-bit soulful boy returns to his star and his rose through a well-chosen death, the long African desert in front of him. At a banal but significant level, it is part of the literary mystique, even after the Algerian war and the loss of empire, to imagine the North African desert as part of the rightful inheritance of the French. French friends often say to Americans that they "feel at home" in the Mahgreb in a way that even the most assured English individuals don't in India—though, rather, it must be said, as Americans feel themselves "at home" in Mexico. (Whether the real inhabitants welcome them quite as keenly as the visitors imagine is, of course, another story.) The North African desert is to the French imagination what the American West is to the American one, the mystical frontier one dreams of, as true in Babar and Saint-Exupéry as in Henri Rousseau.

Yet the insistence on domesticating the desert is not merely imperial. It is also enlightening. As I write these words, as if by magic, my own Parisian theme, Bill Evans's version of the Michel Legrand tune from *Les Demoiselles de Rochefort* (called in English "You Must Believe in Spring") comes on the radio all the way from Paris. How much the melancholy of French *ballades* has done to civilize the jazz tradition, and how much American jazz has done to energize the French *ballade!* All healthy cultures are mongrelized, crossbred between near and far, and though the crossbreeding of the once colonized with the overlord has to be watched with a sense of care, guilt, its happy offspring, should not be banned from our playrooms. The zebra should not be the plaything of the pony, but a pony without a taste for the company of zebras is one that lacks curiosity and imaginative flair.

In the end, the repeated lesson we take from the search for exotic metaphors for domestic experience is that they always end up at home. Our children understand the "hidden messages" of Babar as clearly as they understand its overt content, and they understand as well that the touching absurdity of the elephant's sober pursuit of Frenchness is essentially comic, to be taken as a quixotic quest rather than a narrow object lesson. They understand, too, that the real lessons the book teaches have to do with a life nearer at hand, whether it takes place in the Paris of the 1930s or the New York of the 2000s.

Fig. 6. When danger and disorder loom in Jean de Brunhoff's *Babar the King,* the troubled Babar dreams of a host of winged virtues that chase away strife.

Far more than an allegory of colonialism, the Babar books are a fable of the difficulties of a bourgeois life. "It is hard to raise a family," Babar sighs at one point, and it is true. The city lives on the edge of a desert, and animals wander in and out at random, or at will, and then wander back out again to make cities of their own. The civilizing principle is energetic but essentially comical, solid-looking on the outside but fragile in its foundations, vulnerable to the assaults of rhinoceri (who can reduce it to rubble in a single attack). Even the elephants themselves, for all their learning and sailor suits, can suddenly be turned into slaves through a bad turn of fate. The disorder of natural life is countered by the beautiful symmetries of classical style and the absurd orderliness of domestic life—but we are kidding ourselves if we imagine that we are ever really safe. There are always pirates and flights to other planets. Death is a hunter and a poisoned mushroom away. The only security, the de Brunhoff books propose, lies in our commitment to those graceful winged elephants that, in Babar's dream, chase misfortune away (Fig. 6). Love and Happiness, who are at the heart of the American vision, are, in Babar's dream, mere tiny camp followers. The larger winged elephants, who are at the forefront of this French vision of civilized life, are instead Intelligence, Patience, Learning, and Courage. "Let's work hard and cheerfully and we'll continue to be happy," Babar says, and, though we know that the hunter is still in the woods, it is hard to know what more to add. Even anxious New York parents can safely show their children the murderous page, looking forward to all the life contained in those to come.

Notes

1. Maurice Sendak, "Homage to Babar on His 50th Birthday," *Babar's Anniversary Album*, Random House, 1981, pp. 7–15.
2. Nicholas Fox Weber, *The Art of Babar*, Abrams, 1989, p. 30.

Babar in Progress

The Earliest Drafts
by Jean and Laurent de Brunhoff

CHRISTINE NELSON

Some works of art have become so familiar, so impressed upon memory, that it is difficult to imagine a moment of composition, when a mark was first put to the page. The image of an elephant, standing upright, wearing a green suit and yellow crown, did not, of course, spring into print fully formed. Its existence is the result of a series of individual choices and deliberate acts—a gray suit refashioned in green, the introduction of an elephant queen, an opening scene of mourning altered to one of domestic security. The many manuscript drafts, pencil sketches, and watercolor drawings that survive from the period of Babar's creation provide a remarkably full record of the progression of a classic text—from conception to publication. They allow us to track, in physical form, those moments of decision and inspiration, rejection and embrace of line, word, color, and form by which two men—father and son—brought into being a character and fictional utopia we can almost believe have always been with us.

The creation of Babar is a family story, launched in the twilight of bedtime, like so many children's tales. It entailed a mother's inspiration, the engagement of two young listeners, a father's talent, the support of a family circle of publishers, and the artistic complicity of a son who, years later, chose to give new life to the story he had heard as a little boy. It was in 1930, in a comfortable home just outside Paris, that Cécile de Brunhoff told her sons Laurent and Mathieu, ages five and four (their brother, Thierry, had not yet been born), a story of an unnamed baby elephant who fled the jungle after his mother's death, made his way to a town, and enjoyed the pleasures of the human world, finally returning home with his cousins. There is, of course, no

tangible record of the first oral rendering of this story—delivered simply and without pictures, perhaps elaborated with the delighted participation of the listeners. The boys convinced their father, Jean, to amplify the tale. Cécile de Brunhoff thus ceded her narrative outline to her husband, who took it from there (Fig. 1).

The drafts for the first book by each of *Babar*'s two authors afford an unusual, perhaps unique, opportunity: to witness the making—and remaking—of an iconic fictional world. After Jean de Brunhoff published *Histoire de Babar, le petit éléphant* (The Story of Babar, the Little Elephant) in 1931, he added six titles to the series before his death from tuberculosis at the age of thirty-seven. Of his three sons, twelve-year-old Laurent was the one to whom he unwittingly bequeathed his creation. During his teenage years, Laurent placed his first mark on the series by adding color to a few of the illustrations his father had made for his last two stories—*Babar en famille* (Babar and His Children) and *Babar et le Père Noël* (Babar and Father Christmas), which Jean had drawn in black and white for a British newspaper (Fig. 2). This was the modest start of an intergenerational artistic partnership. By the time Laurent was twenty-one, painting in a studio on the Rue de la Grande Chaumière in Montparnasse, he was ready to add a book of his own to the series: *Babar et ce coquin d'Arthur* (Babar's Cousin: That Rascal Arthur) was published in 1946.

The earliest drawings by Babar's authors, both painters turned storytellers, reveal two very different working methods. Jean developed text and pictures concurrently at every phase of the composition process, sketching in pencil and adding color only in the final stages. Laurent, by contrast, produced explosive swaths of color over the barest hint of graphite, incorporating text only after he had resolved his illustrations. He labored to constrict his near-abstract forms within black-bordered outlines. But a consistent style emerged from such divergent beginnings, fifteen years and a generation apart. When Laurent adopted and revived Babar after the series' wartime hiatus, many readers did not recognize a new hand at work. But in the source works of art the difference is unmistakable. In Jean de Brunhoff's drafts we see the birth of Babar. In Laurent's early *Arthur* sketches, Babar is reborn.

Before Babar

When a story is called for to ease a child's way into sleep, parents generally have no time to craft a well-wrought narrative. The practical rituals of bed-time—the face washing, toothbrushing, and pajama buttoning—often take precedence over careful story plotting. A tale must be conjured on the spot. Thus most parents freely seize elements from traditional stories, adding detail from their children's own lives. Cécile de Brunhoff was no different. She drew on the European stories familiar to her from the work of the Grimm brothers, Hans Christian Andersen, Jean de La Fontaine, Charles Perrault, and Beatrix Potter: tales of talking animals, royal weddings, rags-to-riches transformations, and orphans forced to make their own way in an unfamiliar world. She added references to Paris—a department store elevator, a shopping trip—that her sons would recognize. Having a huge animal undertake these everyday activities introduced an element of delightful absurdity. Her choice of species was not surprising. From Aristotle to Buffon and beyond, humans—even those raised far from Africa or Asia—have been intensely fascinated by elephants. With their physical enormity and attributed intelligence and sagacity, elephants became popular protagonists in children's tales in the decades leading up to the publication of *Babar*. Some figured as pets transported to Europe; some played roles in didactic fables; still others, like Babar, walked upright and wore clothing, standing in for humans.

In "The Elephant's Child," one of his *Just So Stories for Little Children* (1902), Rudyard Kipling used incantatory language to explain how the species acquired its trunk. He included his own black silhouette illustrations (Fig. 3). Like Babar, Kipling's elephant protagonist is young, polite, and innocent, under-takes a transformative journey, acquires new skills while he is away, and returns to change his own society. Another English tale from the same year, Reginald Rigby's *Absurd Story of James* (Fig. 4), recounts (in verse) the sad history of an elephant taken from Uganda to London, painted any number of colors, and, finally, chained up on a lawn in Streatham. ("He spent all the days of his youth / As elephants generally do. / When grown up they caught him, / And somebody

just the very thing he wanted.

"Pack it carefully," he said, and send
Eastern Railway, carriage paid to New R..

(This was not his real name)
Tommy Bates, enclose my card and sen..
to me. And before you send him
round to the place where they paint
peoples trunks & have a nice large T
both sides of him.

All of which they did accordingly

Figs. 3–5. In the early part of the twentieth century, elephant tales for children were popular across many cultures. British examples that pre-date *Babar* include Kipling's 1902 fable "The Elephant's Child" (above), Reginald Rigby's 1905 verse story of "Absurd James" (below), and a homemade book by H. G. Wells (right).

bought him, / But luckily not for the zoo.") James, like Babar, left his native land for a major European city—but his journey did not end nearly as pleasantly. Even H. G. Wells created a homemade book, written and illustrated for a friend's daughter and privately printed in 1928, featuring an elephant bestowed as a gift (Fig. 5). But although some had the power of speech, the elephants in stories like these were intended by their creators to remain, essentially, animals.

A fine example of elephant anthropomorphism, on the other hand, is *Billy's Erdengang: Eine Elephantengeschichte für artige Kinder* (Billy's Time on Earth: An Elephant Story for Well-Behaved Children), a 1902 German picture book. The hero attends school, comes of age, and marries a giraffe, with whom he has hybrid offspring—a *Giraffoelephäntchen*. Billy's upright stance, natty suits, and cosmopolitan mien prefigure Babar (Figs. 6–7). A 1929 Japanese storybook, the upper portion of the volume cut to approximate the shape

of an elephant's head, tells the story of Zōtarō, a mischievous elephant boy who attends school, flies in a green plane (as Babar's equally mischievous cousin Arthur would do in Laurent de Brunhoff's first book), and returns home. Like Dorothy going back to Kansas, Zōtarō learns that "no matter where you go there is no place as pleasant as home." A scene of the happy elephants in Zōtarō's "home country" (Fig. 9) bears a strong resemblance, in both composition and spirit, to that of Babar's triumphant return to the great forest, including the doffing of black hats with trunks (Fig. 8). With the possible

Figs. 6–7. This 1904 German picture book, a precursor to *Babar*, tells the story of a well-dressed elephant who attends school, walks upright, and marries a giraffe. In some illustrations, his green suit matches Babar's.

Figs. 8–9. This 1929 Japanese tale about the adventures of a little elephant boy (below right) includes a scene that resembles Jean de Brunhoff's depiction of Babar's triumphant return to his homeland (below left).

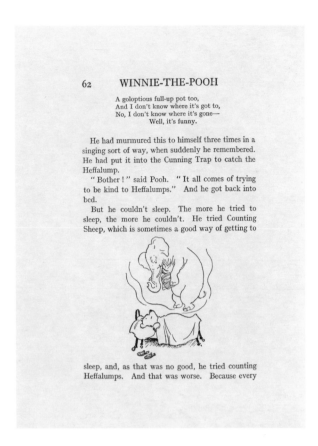

Fig. 10. A. A. Milne's *Winnie-the-Pooh* (1926), a great favorite of the de Brunhoff family, included the bizarre Heffalumps, depicted as elephants by the illustrator, E. H. Shepard.

Fig. 11. Boutet de Monvel's 1896 illustrated history of Joan of Arc has been hailed as a monument in the history of French children's books.

exception of the Kipling story, it is unlikely that the de Brunhoffs were aware of the existence of any of these particular illustrated tales, though additional depictions of elephants abounded in France. But one de Brunhoff family favorite, A. A. Milne's *Winnie-the-Pooh*—published in 1926, just a few years before *Babar*—did include the dream-induced Heffalumps, depicted as elephants by the illustrator E. H. Shepard (Fig. 10).

For *Histoire de Babar*, Jean de Brunhoff provided story, pictures, handwritten text and page layout, thus serving as author, illustrator, and graphic designer. In thinking of his book as a complete package, Jean was in good company. During the late nineteenth century, French artists, poets, and printers had worked together to produce spectacular illustrated books. Most were *éditions de luxe* and not for young readers, though Louis-Maurice Boutet de Monvel's 1896 *Jeanne d'Arc* (Fig. 11) was a notable exception. In the years before *Babar*, some artists endeavored to raise the quality of French illustrated children's literature, producing large-format books of stunning graphic appeal. André Hellé's *Drôles de bêtes* (Figs. 12–13) and Edy Legrand's *Macao et Cosmage* (Fig. 14), both published in the 1910s, were exceptional examples. Hellé's book reflected children's pleasure in large-scale pictures of animals, whereas Legrand's, like the Babar series, explored the nature of *bonheur*, or "well-being," while contrasting nature with civilization. Both, like *Babar*, included text that was handwritten rather

than typeset, and both were large in size—Legrand's 13½ × 13¼ inches (34.5 × 33.6 cm), Hellé's 16½ × 12⅜ inches (42 × 31.4 cm). *Babar* was of similarly generous proportions at 14½ × 10¾ inches (37 × 27 cm). *Macao et Cosmage*, though its illustrations were individually colored (by means of the stenciling process known as pochoir), was much more accessible than a true luxe edition at 20 francs. A dozen years later there were plenty of children's books available in the 10-franc range, which made *Babar* a rather highly priced special book at 35 francs. The offset lithography process employed to print it and other color-

Figs. 12–14. These works by André Hellé (above) and Edy Legrand (below) are fine examples of large-scale, splendidly printed *albums* for French children published in the decades prior to *Babar*. Both included handwritten text.

*Le Roi Apostrophe, Mouté sur son Eléphant,
de Soit la Visite de la Linotte
Lipsi.*

illustrated books of the period permitted the economical production of large print runs, though the initial costs to produce color separations were high.

The Publishing de Brunhoffs

Children's shelves are stocked with published volumes that began, like *Babar,* in the intimacy of family or friendship, from Heinrich Hoffmann's *Struwwelpeter* (1845), invented for the author's own son, to *The Tale of Peter Rabbit* (1901), its origins in the picture letters Beatrix Potter sent to a friend's son. Countless other stories have been chronicled in homemade illustrated books—many quite elaborate, such as *Histoire de Prince Ardelin* (Fig. 15), a 1779 French example in the Morgan's collection created by an unidentified mother to educate and entertain her daughters. Most such efforts never found an audience outside the domestic circle. *Babar* emerged from the nursery and onto the page through the capable hands of Jean de Brunhoff, a skilled painter who discovered—perhaps to his surprise—that he had a narrative as well as a visual gift. But his work might never have reached the public had he not been surrounded and encouraged by an extraordinary family—a father, three siblings, and an influential brother-in-law—of professionals who were devoted to creating, in essence, sophisticated picture books for adults.

Maurice de Brunhoff, Jean's father, published an illustrated edition of the text that has inspired more visual interpretations than any other in the history of Western art: the Bible (Fig. 16). He collaborated with his friend James Tissot (1836–1902), a society painter who experienced a spiritual vision in 1885 and abandoned his fashionable subjects, devoting the latter part of his career exclusively to biblical illustration. After completing a wildly successful New Testament (*La vie de Notre Seigneur Jésus Christ*), published in the 1890s by Mame et fils, Tissot embarked on an Old Testament project. During an 1896 research trip to Jerusalem—his third—he wrote a letter to Maurice full of painterly sensuousness, rhapsodizing about the beauty of the landscape after a rainstorm and the nobility of the barefoot women walking the streets of the old city.[1] Tissot died in 1902 before completing his monumental Old Testament project, but Maurice commissioned various artists to complete and color the preliminary sketches Tissot had left behind. The de Brunhoff–Tissot Old Testament was published in 1904. With over four hundred illustrations, many in color, it was the ultimate picture book.[2]

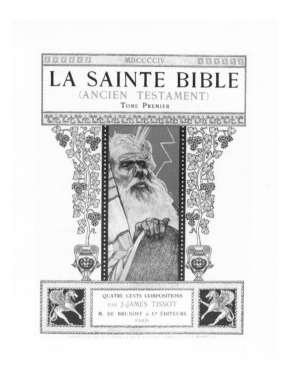

The complex Tissot project behind him, Maurice de Brunhoff witnessed the advent of a major artistic event in Paris and was astute enough to turn it into a publishing opportunity. At the same time that Sergei Diaghilev brought his Ballets Russes to Paris in 1909, Maurice founded the theatrical magazine *Comœdia illustré*. "We immediately realized," he later wrote, "that our young review, created to give the contemporary theatrical and artistic movement the illustrated venue it was lacking, ought to devote an important place to the Ballets Russes and to participate in the veritable revolution it brought to that era in the tradition of dance and particularly in the art of scenic and costume design."[3] Indeed, the Ballets Russes gave Paris not only the astonishing talent of its principal dancer, Vaslav Nijinsky, but also the graphic innovation of its artistic director, Léon Bakst. *Comœdia illustré* began to issue lavish souvenir programs embellished with color-drenched images of designs by artists such as Bakst and Picasso. For the 1911 performance of *Narcisse*[4] at the Thêatre du Châtelet, for example, Maurice framed his program cover with a pattern in gold and placed his firm's name next to an image of Bakst's *divinité inférieure*—its costume even more intensely green than Babar's signature suit (Fig. 17). Once again, the father of Babar's creator had provided a distinctive example of a commercially successful illustrated text.

Jean de Brunhoff's three siblings all followed their father, Maurice, in one way or another, in documenting Parisian art and design in words and pictures. Jacques worked with his father on *Comœdia illustré* before becoming the found-

Figs. 16–17. Maurice de Brunhoff, the father of Jean and grandfather of Laurent, published an elaborate picture Bible in 1904 and later issued illustrated programs for Diaghilev's Ballets Russes. (During this period Maurice spelled the family surname without the *h*.)

ing editor of *Le décor d'aujourd'hui*, a graphically striking magazine of art deco–era home design, in 1933. Michel was named editor in chief of the Paris edition of *Vogue* in 1929, just two years before the publication of *Babar*, while continuing to edit *Le jardin des modes*, another Condé Nast fashion magazine. Jean's eldest sibling, Cosette, a photographer, was the wife of the indefatigable Lucien Vogel, director of *Le jardin des modes* and a highly influential figure in French magazine journalism. He created the splendid periodical *Gazette du bon ton* (1912–25), which brought the worlds of art and fashion together in plates contributed by artists such as the young Raoul Dufy. In 1928 Vogel founded the magazine *VU*, an important early venue for photojournalism and critical photomontage. The photographs in *VU*, printed in rotogravure, often extended to the very edge of the page or crossed the fold, adding to their graphic impact. Laurent de Brunhoff remembers elaborate dinner parties at the Vogels' Paris home, called La Faisanderie, with meals eaten cold because guests had to wait for his Aunt Cosette to photograph them for the pages of *Le jardin des modes*. Thus when Jean de Brunhoff, the youngest of the family and the only one *not* immersed in the publishing world, created an engaging children's book, he was well poised to turn his family story into a commercial success.

It was the family association with *Le jardin des modes* that made possible the publication of *Histoire de Babar* in 1931. The magazine had provided guides to children's fashion in its *albums trimestriels*, and concurrently with *Babar* it published a colorful children's picture book, *La plus vieille histoire du monde*, based on the book of Genesis, printed on linen and illustrated by the artist known as Françoise. *Le jardin des modes* was essentially a style magazine, but perhaps it was not such a great leap from fashion plates to picture books. After all, a great part of the appeal of the early Babar books derived from their graphic splendor, magazinelike size, and graceful integration of text and image. All the de Brunhoffs were skilled, in their own way, in integrating text and image to spectacular effect. Interestingly enough, in August 1930—perhaps just at the time Jean was working up drawings for *Babar*—*Le jardin des modes* published a cover illustration of a woman wearing a solid green hunting suit with a tie and cloche hat (Fig. 18). Babar acquired the gentleman's version of this distinctive attire, by which he would eventually become internationally recognizable (Fig. 19).

Jean de Brunhoff at Work

Provided with the broad story elements by his wife and incited by his two young sons, Jean de Brunhoff turned to his sketchbooks. He added a few key components to Cécile's outline but kept it simple. Working only in graphite,

Le Jardin des Modes

GROUPE DES PUBLICATIONS CONDE NAST

CHASSE GARDÉE
Costume de ARY LISKER

et charge le dromadaire de lui acheter
à la ville de beaux habits de noce.

-41-

incorporating both words and pictures, he built up the structure of a full story-book. With Cécile's encouragement he introduced a new character—a human identified only as *la vieille dame* (the Old Lady), who loved little elephants so much that she gave *bébé éléphant* (the still unnamed protagonist) her purse, allowing him to indulge in urban delights—most important, shopping. The earliest drafts included several episodes that remained in the story, with some adjustments, at every stage of revision to publication: the death of Babar's mother, Babar's escape to the big city, his department store elevator ride, his purchase of new clothes, the arrival of two cousins, the intervention of their mothers, a return to the forest, and a triumphant coronation.

Other story elements, now so familiar to several generations of readers, did not appear in the earliest drafts. There was, for example, no learned professor to provide lessons to the studious Babar. The king of elephants died simply of old age, leaving no heir—there was no poison mushroom, and the king's gruesome green death was not depicted. The old elephant leader (later called Cornelius) was initially unnamed. It was a giraffe, rather than a marabou, that brought news of Babar's whereabouts to his concerned aunts in the great forest (see Nos. 74–78). Perhaps most shocking to those who know Babar's world well, the early drafts did not include the character of Celeste. Two unnamed male cousins (later changed to Arthur and Celeste) ventured into the city to find Babar. The culminating scene of combined marriage and investiture, therefore, was introduced after at least one round of sketches had been completed. In one sketch,

Figs. 18–19. In 1930 the fashion magazine *Le jardin des modes*, which would publish the first Babar book, featured a cover illustration of a woman wearing a green suit. At about the same time, Jean de Brunhoff gave his protagonist a similar ensemble.

rendered with just a few pencil strokes, Babar became king alone (see No. 112). In several early drafts, all three boy cousins were crowned king—"*rois tous les trois*" (see Nos. 102, 113). Jean's initial audience consisted only of his two sons, who probably appreciated this masculine triumvirate.

Once he had sufficiently developed his story, Jean created a small maquette, using sheets of low-quality Johannot et Cie Annonay paper cut down to a page size of 8⅛ × 6⅛ inches (20.5 × 15.5 cm) and folded to approximate a book. In some cases he wrote on separate sheets and then pasted them into the maquette, obscuring earlier drafts he had made on the versos. Written and illustrated in graphite, the maquette included a few watercolor touches and a cover colored in green, yellow, and red crayon, featuring a fully frontal Babar on the upper cover and a rear view (looking much like an elephant backside by Toulouse-Lautrec) on the lower cover (see No. 6). Inside the rear elephant form, he wrote 25 × 32, apparently a proposed page size in centimeters. (The printed pages would be slightly larger at 26.5 centimeters wide and 36.3 high.) He chose to divide some one-page drawings into two-page sequences. Babar's flight from the hunter and arrival in the city, his visit to the department store and elevator ride, and his four-part shopping spree—depicted as single-page episodes in the early drafts—were enlarged to two pages each in the maquette.

As he wrote out the text, he struggled to arrive at an appropriate verb tense, trying out various forms of past tense before settling on the simple present. He provided a sketch for endpapers, retained in the published volume, patterned with an S-chain of trunk-to-tail elephants trekking through a grassy background (see No. 5). The foliage was later eliminated in favor of a solid ground, first painted red but eventually printed in green. He also included a few pages of abstract patterns in green, red, and yellow—perhaps alternate endpapers or color trials—that resembled the curves and loops of cursive script (Fig. 20). On the title page, he boxed in the title and sketched elephants peeking out from behind, a concept that was rejected for the published book (see No. 7). At the foot of the handwritten title page, where the publisher's name would normally appear, he seems to have scrawled *chez nous* (our place)—a reference to the homemade aspect of his booklet.[5] His title page also listed *two* authors: Cécile and Jean de Brunhoff—an acknowledgment of his wife's initial conception. Cécile, however, asked that her name be removed, believing that her husband's artistry far outweighed her own modest contribution to the final work.

By the time Jean put together the maquette, his story had taken shape, but there were major changes in plot, structure, and text to come in the next round of drafts. Returning to his sketchbooks, Jean worked through several revisions, again in pencil, including the addition of the page showing Babar's tutoring session and the change of the informant's species from giraffe to marabou. He subjected the opening and closing pages to a major overhaul. He also made eleven pages of notes on color choices for the final illustrations, using the same type and size of paper he had used for the maquette. It is interesting that color, so integral to the appeal of the published books, was for Jean almost an afterthought. His sketches had all been done in pencil; even the maquette included only sporadic color. (Laurent's approach fifteen years later would be quite the opposite.) Jean's first book included only black, red, green, and yellow—he reserved the use of glorious expanses of blue for his next book, *Le voyage de Babar* (1932). When Jean finally introduced color to his drafts, he planned its use carefully. It was at this point, as he made his notes, that Jean decided on the color of Babar's trademark suit. In the maquette Babar wore a gray suit, while Celeste wore green; Jean's color notes indicate that a department store salesman was also to be dressed in green. On his notes for the color of *E*—the elephant Babar—he wrote *costume gris,* then crossed out *gris* and wrote *vert* (Fig. 21). Crosshatching in the margin suggests a possible texture for the salesman's suit. In the end, Jean dropped green out of the clothing of all characters except that of Babar, thus making him the focal point of any illustration in which he appeared.

His story complete and his color choices made, Jean painted the final illustrations in black ink and watercolor. He copied the text in a plump cursive script that matched the style his sons were being taught in school. The French firm Hachette, which later published the Babar books (beginning in 1936 with *Les vacances de Zéphir*), also issued a series of instructional manuals

Fig. 21. In these early notes, Jean de Brunhoff indicated that Babar would wear a gray suit, but in the final stages of revision he dressed him in green. Page numbers 8 and 9 on this sheet refer to the maquette, not the published book.

for children that included models for handwriting practice (Fig. 22). Though his letterforms were more rounded, Jean's handwritten text resembled the style put forth by the Hachette manuals. Jean cut out his finished illustrations and text and pasted them onto larger sheets, each 14⅛ × 10⅜ inches (36 × 26.5 cm). It was from these assembled mock-ups that the book *Histoire de Babar* was printed in 1931.

The surviving manuscripts do not explain how *bébé éléphant* acquired his name. Could it have been an unwitting (or deliberate) conflation of two or more words—*bébé, père, papa, roi*—"baby," "father," "daddy," "king"—summarizing Babar's roles? In a story about a child elephant who adopts the trappings of European culture, is it significant that his name is just one guttural sound away from *barbare*, the French word for "uncivilized"?[6] Or, in naming his benevolent fictional king, was Jean paying homage to the first Mughal emperor, Babur—sometimes transliterated as *Babar*? It would be nice to think so, but it is unlikely that Jean was aware of Babur's existence. True, Babur's extraordinary journal—the *Baburnama*—had been available in French translation since 1871 and a new English version by Annette Beveridge stirred some interest when it was published in Great Britain in 1912 and 1921—but Babur was simply not well known in France, even among well-educated Parisians, in Jean de Brunhoff's day. E. M. Forster was particularly enamored of Babur upon reading the Beveridge translation and even incorporated him into his 1924 novel, *A Passage to India*. During the seminal scene in the Marabar caves, Forster's Aziz tells his guests that the great emperor "never let go of hospitality and pleasure, and if there was only a little food, he would have it arranged nicely, and if only one musical instrument, he would compel it to play a beautiful tune." Indeed, the words spoken by Forster's Aziz about Babur's delight in lovely food, pleasant music, and a general sense of *bonheur* could easily apply to the elephant king. Perhaps Jean read the French translation of *A Passage to India* when it was serialized (and lavishly praised) in the literary magazine *Revue de Paris* in 1927, a few years before he wrote *Babar*, but that is pure speculation. More likely Jean simply enjoyed the euphony produced by the near rhyme of the two key words in his title *Histoire de Babar*. In any case, by the time he produced the maquette, his protagonist was no longer simply *bébé éléphant*.

Figs. 23–24. This illustration from *Babar* is reminiscent of classic European elephant-hunting narratives, such as the 1862 example on the right.

When he created his maquette, Jean must have felt he was close to finishing the story and layout. After all, he included all the trappings of a published work: cover, title page, even endpapers. And yet he made his most significant changes after completing the maquette—changes that improved the structure of the story and, no doubt, made it much more attractive to both child and adult readers. Neither the early drafts nor the maquette began with the now-familiar image of a baby elephant being rocked in a hammock by his mother but rather with the violent death scene (see Nos. 11–16). These pages, on which a faceless hunter shoots to kill and the infant Babar cries over his mother's body, would have made a jarring opening for a children's book. In articulating the episode, which derived from Cécile's bedtime story and appeared at every stage of composition, Jean drew on familiar depictions of big game hunting. During the nineteenth and early twentieth centuries, many European travelers to Africa returned home to publish swashbuckling accounts of that most prestigious of kills—the elephant—often accompanied by an iconic image of the great beast, centrally portrayed, with the brave hunter in the bottom foreground.[7] (A typical example, the composition of which resembles the *Babar* episode, is shown in Fig. 24.) Some of these narratives included fanciful claims of distraught elephants shedding tears, as Babar does twice. Even the de Brunhoffs had an elephant hunter in the family: Giselle Bunau-Varilla, Jean's glamorous cousin, crossed the Congo in 1929 (the year before Jean began writing *Babar*), hunting elephants with her husband, Mario Rocco, before having a change of heart and settling in Kenya.[8] The elephant hunt was such a staple of colonialist literature that Jean may not have realized the impact his image would have on twentieth-century readers.

Though juvenile literature had long incorporated violence and loss, parental deaths generally happened "off screen," so to speak. (Even the much-discussed death of Bambi's mother in the 1941 Walt Disney film would only be implied by the sound of gunfire.) Still, by making his child hero an animal rather than a human, Jean provided a degree of distance from what would otherwise be unpalatable, or worse—unbearable—to watch: a parent's murder. Writers have long exploited this dichotomy—that animals are both so like and unlike us—to create effective anthropomorphized characters in stories and fables.9

Jean retained the hunting scene but chose to preface it with three pages of domestic bliss. We are introduced to the infant Babar as his mother lovingly rocks him; we then see him playing in the sand along with a community of carefree friends. Jean changed the book's ending substantially as well. The maquette concluded abruptly with the marriage and coronation of Babar and Celeste, the final page showing them facing forward in full-color regalia (see No. 124). Jean eventually decided to dwell on the final party with a bit more leisure, adding an episode in which a dromedary is sent to fetch wedding clothes and depicting the celebration itself in joyous detail. Most importantly, on the final pages, he reversed the orientation of Babar and Celeste, turning them away from the reader and placing them against a black-and-white starry night. He had to work a bit to resolve their posture: in one sketch they are seated, Babar's body inclined toward Celeste and his arm around her shoulder (see No. 122); in another version on the same sketchbook page they stand, his arm quite low around her waist; in a rejected watercolor they stand, Babar's arm around Celeste's shoulders (see No. 121). Jean settled on an elegant stance, the two close against each other but without Babar's awkward forefoot visible. (Jean did allow Babar to put his arm around Celeste, but on an earlier page—when they agree to become king and queen.) On the facing page, Jean repeated the starry scene but without the royal couple (Figs. 25–26).

These key changes at the beginning and end had the pleasing effect of bracketing the story with scenes of domestic comfort. Last-minute additions to the text also emphasized the correspondence between the book's beginning and end. After Babar's mother's death, nature seems to recoil: "The monkey hides, the birds fly away, Babar cries." Jean added a parallel tripartite sentence to the end of his tale, this time expressing a sense of earthly harmony: "The festivities are over, night has fallen, the stars have risen in the sky." Jean de Brunhoff arrived, after much creative labor, at a narrative solution that allowed Babar to begin and end his journey in loving, comfortable relationships. By switching to black and white, documentary fashion, turning the characters' backs on us, and eventually dropping them from the final peaceful

Il tomba doucement comme tombe un arbre.

scene, Jean gracefully distanced his readers from the fictional experience. This technique was so effective that it was adopted a decade later by Antoine de Saint-Exupéry in his popular story *Le petit prince* (The Little Prince). Like *Babar*, Saint-Exupéry's work ends with pages showing the main character from behind against a starry sky, then the landscape alone, this time in black and white (Figs. 27–28).

In addition to the introduction of a new beginning and end, Jean made further changes to the structure of *Babar* before drawing up final watercolors for the printer. A series of small numbered sheets seem to indicate that he considered dividing the story into three chapters: "Babar in the City," "Return to the Forest," and "Babar the King" (Figs. 29–32), but in the end he chose to

Figs. 25–28. Saint-Exupéry's 1943 work *Le petit prince* (below) closed with a pair of illustrations that echoed the ending of *Histoire de Babar.*

present a continuous narrative. The creation of the maquette was a useful exercise that allowed Jean to assess the rhythm of his pages. In the final stages of composition, he increased the number of double-page illustrations (to be printed across the gutter of the book) from two to five. (The maquette's only double-page illustrations, on consecutive spreads, are those of Babar's triumphant return to the forest and the arrival of the animals at the coronation.) He alternated double-page spreads with single-page illustrations, groups of detailed vignettes, and comic-style sequences with no background context. Over several drafts he seemed to struggle with the position and function of his most spectacular double-page spread—that of Babar in his red roadster looping through a fictionalized Marne valley. In an early draft, Babar and his cousins acquired a car (a Peugeot Torpedo) in order to return to the forest—it was not a gift from the Old Lady (see No. 87). In a subsequent draft, the Old Lady gave Babar the car because he was sad, and though he enjoyed driving it, he could not get over his sense of deep longing (see No. 45). After revision, Jean had stripped out the tender language of his early draft and turned the car scene into one of pure graphic beauty and material fulfillment. The Old Lady simply gives Babar a car. In fact, "she gives him anything he wants."

Jean continued to pare away superfluous language to achieve the directness and simplicity that distinguish his published work. Time and again he removed words and phrases that sentimentalized the story, trusting his illustrations instead to supply emotional weight. "After the death of his mother, too sad to stay in the forest, Baby Elephant runs away" was changed to "Babar runs away because he is afraid of the hunter." Babar's sadness and even his mother's death are not mentioned in the published version of this sentence. Instead his loneliness is conveyed graphically through his physical posture and his lowly, isolated position on the page as he looks up at the big city (see

No. 18). Compare Jean de Brunhoff's restraint to the following overt statement made by Timothy Mouse, the sidekick of the most famous of American fictional elephants, Walt Disney's Dumbo: "Suppose you was torn away from your mother when you was just a baby? Nobody to tuck you in at nights, no warm, soft, caressin' trunk to snuzzle into? How would you like to be left out alone in a cold, cruel, heartless world?"[10] Though Babar, like Dumbo, finds comfort in an affectionate companion of a different species—the Old Lady—neither she nor the book's narrator articulates the orphan's grief.

Because he treated his work as a unified whole rather than a story with tacked-on pictures (or vice versa), Jean could see clearly where word or image might need to be tweaked in order to further the narrative most efficiently and effectively. In an early draft, Babar moves in with the Old Lady because "he loves her so much," but in the published story he simply "now lives at the Old Lady's house." Their intimacy is represented through pictures of their everyday activities—exercise, dining, and walks—rather than verbally. When Babar's cousins arrive in the city, an early draft explains their motivation: "Arthur and Celeste ran away from the forest to find Babar because they very much wanted to see him again and to play with him." In the final text, the cousins simply show up and rush off to buy clothes and eat cake. Their happiness in seeing Babar again is conveyed in the image of their joyous physical reunion. And when Babar finally leaves the Old Lady—certainly the most overtly sentimental episode in the book—he hugs her "one last time" in an early draft. Jean deleted those words in favor of a highly charged image of their final embrace. But perhaps the most interesting of all Jean's rejected texts appears in rough form on the verso of one of the drawings. When Babar's aunts arrive in the city, angry but relieved, they scold Arthur and Celeste like good French mothers and prepare to take them back home. But Jean apparently toyed with the idea of having the aunts also confront Babar as a species traitor. After all, he had lost his mother to an evil hunter and then turned around and adopted the ways of humankind. In Jean's obsolete text, the aunts reproach Babar, "How can you live among men? Have you forgotten that your mother was killed?" (see No. 83).

The drafts also show a softening of Babar's tendency toward pomposity. In the published book, Babar visits a photographer to document his newly acquired wardrobe. In early drafts, Babar presents a signed copy of the photograph to the Old Lady upon bidding her farewell (see Nos. 85–86). Though the bestowal of a photograph can be a sign of affection, in these sketches it smacks of self-importance, and Jean was probably wise to delete it. In the maquette, the newly vested Babar extends a written invitation to the animal community, calling himself Babar I and employing the royal plural: "We,

Babar I, king of the elephants, invite you to attend our marriage to our cousin Celeste and the festivities of our coronation" (see No. 105). In the final version, Babar instead sends birds as his emissaries, a less grandiose, more poetic way to issue a forestwide invitation.

In his seminal work *Art and Illusion*, E. H. Gombrich discussed the "sublime simplification" that artists may employ to render the complexity of facial expression with a limited repertoire of lines. He reproduced a page from *Histoire de Babar* to illustrate how Jean de Brunhoff "with a few hooks and dots could impart whatever expression he desired even to the face of an elephant, and he could make his figures almost speak merely by shifting those conventional signs which do duty for eyes in children's books."[11] The illustration he selected to make this point was that of Babar's aunts depicted with jagged Vs above their eyes to signify their anger (see No. 79). The drafts for *Babar* make clear that such seemingly effortless effects were often the result of studied labor. In the maquette, for example, the aunts' "eyebrows" are not yet Vs— they are closer to *inverted* Vs—and as a result the sense of parental censure is not as great (see No. 81). Close examination of Jean's many surviving draft pages reveal countless such subtle adjustments that contributed to the effectiveness of his final product.

A dramatic example may be seen in the series of sketches for the Old Lady's balcony scene (see Nos. 89–93). In early drafts, we see her watch her "little Babar" depart from various vantage points. In one sketch she stands in the background as the elephants pass in front of her. In another she appears on the balcony in the lower right corner. In the maquette, her presence is almost insignificant at the upper right of the page with Babar's aunts instead taking graphic precedence. Still two more sketches come close to the final composition, in which the Old Lady stands on the balcony in the lower left corner, slim but solid and dark, her sadness palpable as the elephants depart up a long tree-lined street. The exaggerated perspective emphasizes the increasing distance between her and Babar. Her placement in the left foreground allows the illustration to be read in narrative form, from left to right. And the steep diagonal axis mirrors the scene in which Babar first arrived in the big city he is now leaving.

Another challenge Jean faced was to resolve the relative size of the various characters. The arrival of Babar's cousins, for example, presented some difficulty (see Nos. 55–73). Celeste and Arthur must initially seem small and innocent, unlike the mature and sophisticated Babar, and yet Celeste must almost immediately be perceived as an age-appropriate mate for him. When the cousins first appear running down a city street, they are tiny in comparison to Babar's upright bulk. In the published book, Jean retained this strong distinction. But in the maquette and several sketches for the subsequent episodes, Babar and his cousins are drawn in approximately equal proportions. A few sketches show three elephants facing away from the reader in a balanced embrace (see Nos. 65–66), but in his final watercolor, Jean switched their orientation and drew the substantial and fully clothed Babar facing the reader and towering over his two unclothed, immature visitors, like an imposing Uncle Lucien Vogel welcoming young Laurent and Mathieu de Brunhoff to Sunday lunch. Jean worked through several pencil sketches of the cousins' department store visit and arrival at the pastry shop. By the time the three are seated and enjoying éclairs, Jean has transformed Celeste from little girl to maternal figure. A subtle but key change to the text emphasized Babar's emotional distance from his cousins. In the maquette, his aunts travel to the city to retrieve Arthur, Celeste, and Babar: they will leave "tomorrow, no later." But in the final text, Babar makes his own choice to join them on the journey home. Unlike his cousins, he is a fully formed adult, now empowered to make his own decisions. It simply wouldn't do for the future king to return home at the behest of a couple of angry aunts. For his coming of age tale to end appropriately, he must have the autonomy to determine his own final course.

The maquette closes with an announcement to the reader: *Here ends the story of Babar, the little elephant, but you can find out what happened to him if you read the story of Babar the king.* Jean also completed a watercolor drawing showing Babar, Celeste, and Arthur, all clothed, riding triumphantly atop three unclothed elephants, with the caption *In another book we will explain how their adventures continued* (see No. 125). The published book did not, in fact, include an advertisement for a sequel, but these drafts reveal that Jean was already looking forward to writing one. He surely never imagined that there would eventually be more than forty.

Laurent de Brunhoff's First *Babar*

Histoire de Babar is a book about coming of age, behaving properly, living well, and assuming responsibility—in short, an adult story, as befit its author, a mature married man raising a family. Babar's childhood was abruptly foreshortened. Jean de Brunhoff gave him just one moment of sleepy comfort and one afternoon of carefree play. His adolescent rebellion was limited to a wild ride on a department store elevator before he donned a dinner suit and chatted with humans in his benefactress's parlor. In *Babar et ce coquin d'Arthur*, by contrast, Laurent de Brunhoff—barely emerged from the teenage years himself—put forth a tale of youthful adventure. While Babar's great spree involved the purchase of a conservative suit of clothes, Arthur is drawn instead to an enormous airplane. Laurent chose to color the plane with a flat expanse of green exactly the shade of Babar's outfit—a chromatic reference that linked the two cousins. Having lived in intimate proximity to Celesteville since the age of five, Laurent had no trouble choosing the protagonist for his first book in the series. It would be *ce coquin d'Arthur*—that rascal Arthur, older than Babar's little triplets yet not quite a man. When he applied "Babar green" to Arthur's airplane, Laurent understood the desires of his audience. What would young readers find more exciting—a confining three-piece suit or an illicit ride on a spanking aircraft?

Laurent chose to diminish Babar's importance and allow his young cousin's high energy to propel the narrative. Indeed, when he submitted drawings to the publisher, Hachette, Laurent entitled the book simply *Ce coquin d'Arthur* (see Nos. 126–27). The publisher may have prevailed on him to include Babar's name in the title to emphasize continuity with the Jean de Brunhoff series—probably a wise choice from a marketing point of view. Arthur—like Curious George, also conceived in Paris during the 1940s—is caught in that transitional stage somewhere between childhood and maturity. Poor kid—too fat to travel in the overhead cable car with Babar's children but not sufficiently mature to be granted full parity with his adult cousins. Laurent communicates this awkwardness graphically. In a sketch for the cable car scene (see Nos. 136, 139), Arthur is confined below in a conventional train with Babar and Celeste, dramatically separated from the triplets, who get to "fly" above—what fun for them! Though stuck with the grown-ups, Arthur shows that he is still full of silliness by making faces at the children above, their tiny trunks hanging down. The physical gulf between them—a space left blank for text—emphasizes their enforced segregation. No wonder Arthur sneaks off for his own high ride when he gets the chance.

Though Laurent had been painting mostly abstract canvases before he resumed the family saga, his training at the Académie de la Grande Chaumière in Montparnasse did include traditional figure drawing. Both approaches came into play as he composed *Arthur*. Some fifty-three preliminary watercolor sketches, twenty-seven black line drawings, and twenty-six finished works for the book document Laurent's process. In them we can trace a dramatic shift from abstraction, which came naturally, to narrative illustration, which required some suppression of his creative energy. A close look at a detail of the figures of Babar and Arthur from the double-spread depiction of the Celesteville train station provides a clear record of the steps Laurent took to finalize his work (Fig. 33). More versions survive for this episode than for any other in the book—evidence of the care Laurent took to compose and refine the scene. The fact that today, a full six decades after he painted these pages, Laurent still remembers the physical act of working on them is testa-

ment to his deep engagement with this particular composition. Despite having been created for a storybook, the train station scene is a complete painting in its own right, like all of Laurent's double-page spreads. There are eight of them in *Arthur* to Jean's five in *Histoire de Babar*.

Unlike his father, Laurent developed his story primarily through pictures, not words, and certainly not by integrating words with pictures. He did not retain any textual drafts that would allow us to trace his process of composition. But it is clear from the many extant drawings that he inserted text into the page layouts in the final stages. His earliest sketches were made in bold strokes of watercolor over a welter of faint pencil lines. He made three such studies for the illustration of Babar and Arthur at the Celesteville train station. At this early stage Laurent excluded detail, defining spaces and relationships with broad brushstrokes of intense color. He then set out to demarcate the figures, sometimes applying black ink directly over the watercolor. The printer then required a black-line drawing of the entire page to facilitate color registration. (Jean de Brunhoff, too, had employed this process beginning in 1933 with *Le roi Babar*.) Where he wished to revise his line, Laurent applied white gouache, much like correcting fluid, over the ink. He then submitted the black-line drawing to the printer, who produced from it a black-line proof and

Fig. 33. To create illustrations for publication, Laurent de Brunhoff worked first in watercolor over a pencil sketch, then produced a black-line drawing from which the printer derived a proof, and finally applied watercolors to the proof. The printer handled color separation.

Figs. 34–35. Laurent de Brunhoff was forced to restrain his natural brushwork in order to prepare his drawings for publication. He initially rendered this tree in loose brushstrokes but added a black outline and simplified the color scheme to conform to the style of previous editions in the series.

returned it to Laurent. Laurent painted his final color on the proof. From this completed artwork, it was up to the printer to divide the page into its component colors, each of which was printed separately by means of offset lithography. Laurent's colored black-line proofs served as a key for the printer, who had to provide some level of translation to prepare the press plates. For example, in the images of the elephants' heads, a bit of variegation was added that did not appear in Laurent's drawing. The blue of the sky was sometimes intensified beyond Laurent's wishes, though the fading of the watercolors over time makes it difficult to assess to what degree such adjustments were made. Laurent also provided instructions to indicate where he wished flat color to be printed and where he preferred a screen. Babar's coat and hat (and Arthur's plane) were always printed in flat green, even though the source watercolors reveal some modulation. His gray skin, however, was achieved through a screen of black dots. Some trees were printed in flat green, others with screens of various percentages of green to vary the density of the landscape.

In his eight double-page spread illustrations, Laurent indulged his painterly bent. Consider, for example, the exquisite tree on the right-hand side of the scene in which Arthur awakens to discover that monkeys have uncoupled his train car (see detail in Figs. 34–35; full image in Nos. 176–77). Laurent rendered a lush landscape in which the presence of a few little animals barely registers at first glance. For printing, the free brushstrokes with their subtle blend of greens and blues had to be reduced to a stark black outline and the color broken down into a plane of green dots over a hint of yellow. As he revised, Laurent strengthened the narrative quality of the drawing by emphasizing the presence of Arthur and his simian tormentors. On the one hand, to conform to his father's style, Laurent had to repress his own. On the other hand, what his work may have lost during the revision process—some of its energy and freedom—it gained in humor and narrative force. While the humor in *Histoire de Babar* derived in large part from a sense of incongruity and absurdity, *Arthur* contains more moments of unabashed joy: the delight of hopping on a big plane, clowning around with baby kangaroos, and crossing an improvised bridge of hippopotami.

Despite Laurent's persistence in defining himself as a painter rather than a storyteller, his first book is characterized by momentum and suspense. While he clearly gloried in making big paintings that would fill two pages, he understood the importance of graphic pacing. Like his father, he alternated double-page spreads with smaller vignettes and several comic-style sequences to portray the quick passage of time. On several preliminary drawings, he made pencil notes to himself to alter a page's composition for improved narrative effect. In a study for the episode in which Arthur visits the airfield, Laurent placed him on the far right corner of the page, admiring the plane from afar. Laurent made a note to himself to place Arthur next to the plane instead (see No. 147). In the published illustration, we see that Laurent indeed changed Arthur's position and reduced his size, emphasizing his engagement with the plane but also making the visual narrative read more effectively from left to right. In a sketch for the following pages, on which the great green plane takes off with Arthur on its wing, Laurent made a note to himself to make the aircraft *plus petit*—"smaller," to exaggerate its recession into the horizon and to create a dramatic diagonal axis from the crowd of big elephants massed in the lower left corner (Fig. 37; see also No. 151). In the accompanying text, he heightened the suspense with eyewitness patter: "He'll fall off! He'll surely fall off!—No! He seems to be holding on fast!—He must be holding on by his trunk!"

When the plane takes off with Arthur on its wing, a helpful passenger pulls him in through the window. Laurent tried both a "north" and "south" view of chubby Arthur in the window frame—very similar to that of Winnie-the-Pooh stuck in the entrance to Rabbit's den—and settled on the south view (see Nos. 154–55). Ejected from the plane by the angry rhinoceros pilot, Arthur parachutes into the land of kangaroos (who also appear as "Strange Animals" in *Winnie-the-Pooh*), far from the safety of Baribarbotton,[12] the seaside retreat of Babar and his family. Before *Arthur*, airplanes figured prominently in children's stories conceived in France, the cradle of flight. Edy Legrand's *Macao et Cosmage* (1919) included a scene with a plane receding

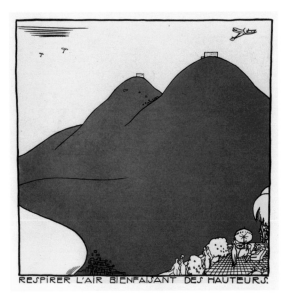

RESPIRER L'AIR BIENFAISANT DES HAUTEURS.

Figs. 36–37. In *Macao et Cosmage* (1919; left), Edy Legrand depicted a small plane in the distance in the upper right corner of the page, as Laurent de Brunhoff did several decades later in *Babar et ce coquin d'Arthur.*

Fig. 38. In a draft of *Le petit prince,* Saint-Exupéry sketched his narrator, a pilot, and his downed plane. The published book, however, did not include any images of the narrator.

Les bêtes sauvages trouvent Doudou si gentille et si douce
qu'elles ne lui font aucun mal.
Elles deviennent vite ses amies.
Pendant que l'éléphant l'aide
à construire une maison au bord de la mer,
Touf et les oiseaux lui font de la musique.

into the upper right corner of the page, similar to Arthur's getaway craft (Fig. 36). Saint-Exupéry, a daring flier himself, used a plane crash as a vehicle to set up his narrator's encounter with the Little Prince. Though neither the aircraft nor the narrator are pictured in the book, Saint-Exupéry depicted them in a preliminary sketch (Fig. 38). *Doudou s'envole*, a colorful storybook published in France in 1934, a dozen years before *Arthur*, also told the story of a young protagonist whose plane, detached from a carnival ride, takes her to a land of unusual animals, including elephants (Figs. 39–40).

Like Babar in his first storybook, Arthur not only enjoys his time away from family in an alien land, he also benefits from it by having fun, making new friends, and gaining independence. But his journey, unlike Babar's, is the result of a youthful transgression rather than a family tragedy. Babar's trajectory from beloved infant to benevolent monarch was an epic one. Though he returned to his homeland, he had suffered deep loss, come of age, and learned the ways of responsible adulthood. Arthur, despite facing such perils as forced skydiving and snapping crocodiles, simply enjoys an afternoon's lark. He remains forever the same fun-loving age. After a joyful reunion with Babar and Celeste, he falls exhaustedly into bed. Laurent's final page, in which a maternal Celeste brings pajamas to the sleeping Arthur, recalls the now iconic illustration of Peter Rabbit tucked into a similar bed as his mother ministers to

Figs. 39–40. During the first decades of flight, children's stories that featured airplane rides included the Japanese story shown in Fig. 9 and this 1934 French example about a little girl whose carnival plane goes astray, depositing her in a land of friendly animals.

Figs. 41–42. Like the *Peter Rabbit* storybook adored by the de Brunhoff children, *Babar et ce coquin d'Arthur* closed with a comforting nighttime scene in which a mischievous but beloved child is put to bed.

him with a cup of chamomile tea (Figs. 41–42). Both Peter and Arthur deserved a scolding, but both were well-loved. *The Tale of Peter Rabbit* was a family favorite in the de Brunhoff household. The tender ending that Laurent de Brunhoff created for his first book thus circled back to his own childhood of comforting bedtimes full of stories from favorite books and, one extraordinary night, a new tale about a baby elephant who was born in the great forest, and whose mother loved him very much.

Notes

1. Letter from James Tissot to Maurice de Brunhoff, dated Jerusalem, 6 April 1896. Collection of The Morgan Library & Museum.

2. Copy 1 of the de Brunhoff–Tissot Old Testament, in an elaborate binding by Edouard Pagnant, is in the collection of The Morgan Library & Museum. It includes Maurice de Brunhoff's detailed explanation of the completion of the illustrations after Tissot's death.

3. Maurice and Jacques de Brunhoff, in the preface to *Collection des plus beaux numéros de Comœdia illustré et des programmes consacrés aux Ballets & Galas Russes depuis le début à Paris, 1909–1921*. Paris: M. de Brun[h]off, [1922?].

4. Music by Nicolai Tcherepnin; choreography by Michel Fokine.

5. Laurent de Brunhoff speculates that this text instead reads *Chessy*, the name of the home of his maternal grandparents, the Sabourauds, where *Babar* was conceived.

6. Both Ariel Dorfman and Nicholas Fox Weber have pointed out that Babar's name incorporates the sounds of the French words for "baby" and "father." (Fox Weber, *The Art of Babar*, Abrams, 1989, p. 27. Dorfman, *The Empire's Old Clothes: What the Lone Ranger, Babar, and Other Innocent Heroes Do to Our Minds*, Pantheon Books, 1983, p. 50.) Claire-Lise Malarte-Feldman and Jack Yeager noted the similarity between *Babar* and *barbare* ("Babar and the French Connection: Teaching the Politics of Superiority and Exclusion" in *Critical Perspectives on Postcolonial African Children's and Young Adult Literature*, Meena Khorana, ed., Greenwood Press, 1998, p. 72).

7. Roualeyn Gordon Cumming's *Five Years of a Hunter's Life in the Far Interior of South Africa* (1850) was perhaps the best known of such narratives. See Nigel Rothfels, "Killing Elephants: Pathos and Prestige in the Nineteenth Century" in *Victorian Animal Dreams: Representations of Animals in Victorian Literature and Culture*, Deborah Denenholz Morse and Martin A. Danahay, eds., Ashgate, 2007, and his article "Why Look at Elephants?" in *Worldviews*, vol. 9, no. 2, 2005. I am grateful to Dr. Rothfels for calling my attention to various images and accounts of the elephant hunt.

8. Sirocco, the house built for Giselle and Mario in Naivasha, Kenya, is now occupied by their daughter Oria and her husband, Iain Douglas-Hamilton, leaders in animal conservation and founders of the organization Save the Elephants.

9. This phenomenon was most famously discussed by John Berger in his essay "Why Look at Animals?" in *About Looking*, Pantheon Books, 1980, pp. 1–26.

10. Walt Disney's *Dumbo* was released in the United States in 1941, a decade after the publication of *Babar*. It was released in France in 1947. In 1936 Disney's Silly Symphonies also produced a short film, *Elmer Elephant*, which, like *Dumbo*, is a typically American story about the importance of self-esteem.

11. E. H. Gombrich, *Art and Illusion: A Study in the Psychology of Pictorial Representation*, Pantheon Books, 1960, pp. 334–35.

12. *Baribarbotton* is Laurent de Brunhoff's play on the words *barrir*, "to trumpet" (the sound made by an elephant), and *barbotter*, "to splash around"—an appropriate invented place name for a seaside resort for elephants. It also contains the name *Babar*.

Reproduced in this section are virtually all surviving draft pages of text and illustrations for Jean de Brunhoff's first book, *Histoire de Babar, le petit éléphant* (1931), grouped by subject to show the development of each episode in the story. Four types of drawings are shown: pencil sketches, most incorporating draft text; pages from de Brunhoff's maquette (a small mock-up of the entire book); pages from the printer's dummy comprising finished watercolors and handwritten text pasted to backings; and variant watercolors. In the few cases in which the final watercolors are not in the Morgan's collection, pages from the first printed edition have been reproduced instead.

Transcriptions and translations of all text have been provided. The French text (as published in the first edition) appears first along with an English translation, adapted from the 1933 version by Merle Haas. Following the published version of the text are transcriptions and translations of all Jean de Brunhoff's draft text. To increase readability, diacritical marks and essential punctuation have been included here, even if absent or ambiguous in the original manuscripts. Deleted text is supplied, with the exception of simple false starts and corrected verb endings (for example, de Brunhoff changed a verb from *promenait* to *promène* by writing the final *e* over *ait*; this has not been recorded in the transcription). Erased text has not been transcribed. Where a word or portion of a word is clearly missing or incorrect, bracketed text is supplied for clarification.

Jean de Brunhoff's

Histoire de Babar, le petit éléphant

Introducing Babar

1

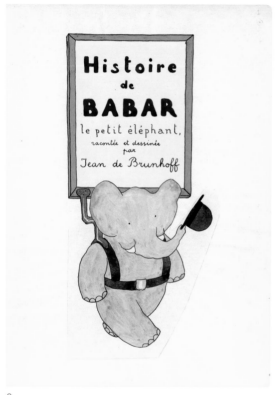

3

2

1. Dummy for cover.

2. Variant illustration for cover.

3. Maquette, front cover.

4. Dummy for endpapers.

5. Maquette, front endpaper.

6. Maquette, back cover.

7. Maquette, title page.
Histoire de Babar le petit Eléphant / raconté par Cécile et Jean de Brunhoff / chez nous [or Chessy?]

The Story of Babar, the Little Elephant / told by Cecile and Jean de Brunhoff / our place [or Chessy?]

4

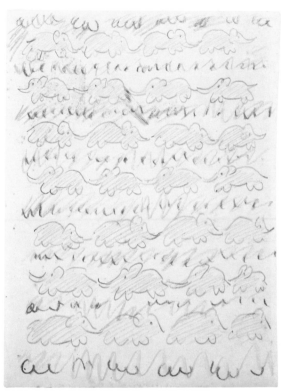

5

6

7

An Elephant Is Born

Dans la grande forêt 3
un petit éléphant est né.
Il s'appelle Babar.
Sa maman l'aime beaucoup.
Pour l'endormir,
elle le berce avec sa trompe
en chantant tout doucement.

-3-

8

8. Dummy for p. 3.
Dans la grande forêt un petit éléphant est né. Il s'appelle Babar. Sa maman l'aime beaucoup. Pour l'endormir, elle le berce avec sa trompe en chantant tout doucement.

In the great forest a little elephant is born. His name is Babar. His mother loves him very much. She rocks him to sleep with her trunk while singing softly to him.

9. First edition, pp. 4–5.
Babar a grandi. Il joue maintenant avec les autres enfants éléphants. C'est un des plus gentils. C'est lui qui creuse le sable avec un coquillage.

Babar has grown bigger. He now plays with the other little elephants. He is one of the sweetest ones. He is the one digging sand with a shell.

10. Study for pp. 4–5.
Les petits enfants éléphants vivant heureux chez eux dans la grande forêt.

The little elephants living happily at home in the great forest.

Babar a grandi. Il joue maintenant
C'est un des plus gentils. C'est lui

avec les autres enfants éléphants.
qui creuse le sable avec un coquillage.—

-4-

-5-

9

Les petits enfants éléphants vivent heureux
toujours dans la grande forêt.—

10

The Hunter

Babar se promène très heureux sur le dos de sa maman, quand un vilain chasseur, 6 caché derrière un buisson, tire sur eux.

-6-

11

Le chasseur a tué la maman. Le singe se cache, les oiseaux s'envolent, Babar pleure. Le chasseur court pour attraper le pauvre Babar.

-7-

12

11. Dummy for p. 6.
Babar se promène très heureux sur le dos de sa maman, quand un vilain chasseur, caché derrière un buisson, tire sur eux.

Babar is riding happily on his mother's back when a wicked hunter, hidden behind a bush, shoots at them.

12. Dummy for p. 7.
Le chasseur a tué la maman. Le singe se cache, les oiseaux s'envolent, Babar pleure. Le chasseur court pour attraper le pauvre Babar.

The hunter has killed Babar's mother. The monkey hides, the birds fly away, Babar cries. The hunter runs up to catch poor Babar.

13. Maquette, p. 1 (corresponding to pp. 6–7 of published book).
Babar le petit éléphant se promène un jour très heureux sur le dos de sa maman quand lorsqu'un chasseur à l'affût tire et tue maman éléphant. Babar pleure.

Babar the little elephant is riding happily on his mother's back one day when a hunter shoots from a blind and kills Mother Elephant. Babar cries.

14. Study for pp. 6–7.
Madame Eléphant et Bébé Eléphant se promènent dans la forêt très heureux. Mais le vilain chasseur tire et tue Maman Eléphant. Bébé éléphant pleure.

Mrs. Elephant and Baby Elephant are walking happily along in the forest. But the evil hunter shoots and kills Mother Elephant. Baby Elephant cries.

15. Study for p. 6.

16. Variant drawing and text for pp. 6–7.
Maman Eléphant et Bébé Eléphant se promènent dans la forêt très heureux. Mais le vilain chasseur tire et tue Maman Eléphant. Bébé éléphant pleure.

Mother Elephant and Baby Elephant are walking happily along in the forest. But the evil hunter shoots and kills Mother Elephant. Baby Elephant cries.

13

14

15

16

A Long Journey

17

18

17. Dummy for p. 8.

Babar se sauve parce qu'il a peur du chasseur. Au bout de quelques jours, bien fatigué, il arrive près d'une ville . . .

Babar runs away because he is afraid of the hunter. After several days, very tired indeed, he comes to a town . . .

18. Dummy for p. 9.

Il est très étonné parce que c'est la première fois qu'il voit tant de maisons.

He is amazed because this is the first time that he has seen so many houses.

19. Maquette, pp. 2–3 (corresponding to pp. 8–9 of published book).

Babar tout triste se sauve loin de la forêt et du chasseur. Au bout de quelques jours il arrive près d'une ville. / Il est très étonné parce que c'est la première fois qu'il voit tant de maisons.

Very sad indeed, Babar runs far away from the forest and from the hunter. After several days, he comes to a town. / He is amazed because this is the first time he has seen so many houses.

20. Study for pp. 8–9.

Bébé éléphant se sauve et marche longtemps, longtemps. Très fatigué il arrive ~~dans~~ près d'une ville. Il est très étonné parce que c'est la 1e fois qu'il voit tant de maisons.

Baby Elephant runs away and walks for a long, long time. Feeling very tired, he comes ~~into~~ to a town. He is amazed because this is the 1st time he has seen so many houses.

21. Study for pp. 8–9.

Après la mort de sa mère, trop triste pour rester dans la forêt, Bébé Eléphant se sauve et court longtemps, longtemps. Très fatigué il arrive près d'1 ville. Il est très étonné parce que c'est la 1e fois qu'il voit tant de maisons.

After his mother's death, too sad to remain in the forest, Baby Elephant flees and runs for a long, long time. Feeling very tired, he comes to a town. He is amazed because this is the 1st time he has seen so many houses.

22. Study for pp. 8–9.

Après la mort de sa mère, trop triste pour rester dans la forêt, Bébé Eléphant se sauve et court longtemps, longtemps. Très fatigué, il arrive près d'une ville. Il est très étonné parce que c'est la première fois qu'il voit tant de maisons. ~~Il s'assied~~

After his mother's death, too sad to remain in the forest, Baby Elephant flees and runs for a long, long time. Feeling very tired, he comes to a town. He is amazed because this is the first time he has seen so many houses. ~~He sits down~~

19

20

21

22

Welcome to the City

23. Dummy for p. 10.

Que de choses nouvelles! Ces belles avenues! Ces autos et ces autobus! Pourtant ce qui intéresse le plus Babar, ce sont deux messieurs qu'il rencontre dans la rue. / Il pense: « Vraiment ils sont très bien habillés. Je voudrais bien avoir aussi un beau costume. . . . » Mais comment faire???

So many things are new to him! The broad streets! The automobiles and buses! However, Babar is especially interested in two gentlemen he notices on the street. / He says to himself: "Really, they are very well dressed. I would like to have some fine clothes, too. . . . " But how can he do it???

24. First edition, p. 11.

Heureusement une vieille dame très riche, qui aimait beaucoup les petits éléphants, comprend en le regardant qu'il a envie d'un bel habit. Comme elle aime faire plaisir elle lui donne son porte-monnaie. Babar lui dit: « Merci, Madame. »

Luckily, a very rich old lady who has always been fond of little elephants understands right away that he is longing for a fine suit. As she likes to make people happy, she gives him her purse. Babar says to her, "Thank you, ma'am."

25. Maquette, pp. 4–5 (corresponding to pp. 10–11 of published book).

Dans la rue il voit Babar voit des messieurs. Il trouve qu'ils sont vraiment très bien habillés. Il voudrait bien avoir aussi un beau costume—mais comment ? faire? / Heureusement une vieille dame très riche qui aimait beaucoup les petits éléphants voyant son embarras lui donne son porte-monnaie. Babar lui dit: « Merci, madame. »

He sees Babar sees some gentlemen on the street. He thinks they are really very well dressed. He, too, would very much like to have such fine clothes—but how? can he do it? / Luckily, a very rich old lady who has always been fond of little elephants sees his problem and gives him her purse. Babar says to her, "Thank you, ma'am."

26. Study for pp. 10–11.

Il rencontre dans la rue des messieurs. Il trouve leurs costumes bien beaux! Il voudrait bien avoir aussi un beau costume aussi mais comment faire? Heureusement une vieille dame qui aimait beaucoup les petits éléphants lui donne son porte-monnaie. Il lui dit « merci beaucoup Madame. »

Babar meets some gentlemen on the street. He thinks their suits are very handsome! He, too, would very much like to have such fine clothes too—but how can he do it? Luckily, a very rich old lady who has always been fond of little elephants gives him her purse. Babar says to her, "Thank you very much, ma'am."

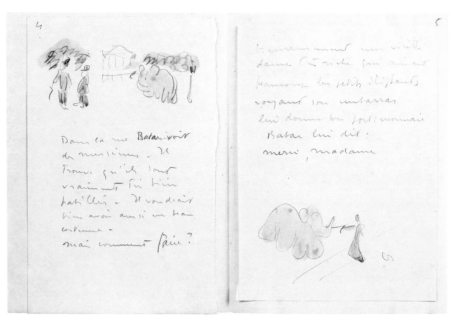

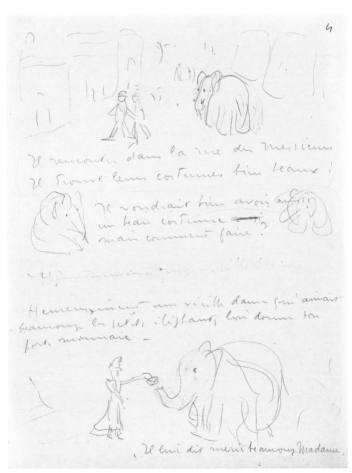

An Elevator Ride

27. Dummy for p. 12.

Sans perdre une minute Babar va dans un grand magasin. Il entre dans l'ascenseur. Il trouve si amusant de monter et de descendre dans cette drôle de boite, qu'il monte dix fois tout en haut, descend dix fois tout en bas. Il allait continuer quand le groom de l'ascenseur lui dit: « Ce n'est pas un joujou, monsieur l'éléphant, maintenant il faut sortir pour acheter ce que vous voulez, justement voilà le chef de rayon. »

Without wasting any time, Babar goes into a big store. He enters the elevator. It is such fun to ride up and down in this funny box, that he rides all the way up ten times and all the way down ten times. He was going to continue but the elevator boy finally says to him: "This is not a toy, Mr. Elephant. You must get out and do your shopping. Look, here is the floorwalker."

28. Dummy for p. 13.

29. Maquette, pp. 6–7 (corresponding to pp. 12–13 of published book).

~~Vite il va~~ Babar va vite dans un grand magasin. Il entre dans l'ascenseur. Il trouve si amusant de monter et de descendre dans cette drôle de boîte, qu'il mont[e] 10 fois tout en haut, descend 10 fois tout en bas. Il allait continuer quand le monsieur [inserted: le groom de l'ascenseur, garçon de l'ascenseur] qui fait marcher l'ascenseur lui dit: « Ce n'est pas un joujou, monsieur l'éléphant, maintenant il faut sortir pour acheter ce que vous voulez. Justement voilà le chef de rayon. »

~~Quickly he goes~~ Quickly Babar goes into a big store. He enters the elevator. It is such fun to ride up and down in this funny box that he goes all the way up 10 times and all the way down 10 times. He was going to continue when the man who runs elevator [inserted: the elevator operator, the elevator boy] says to him, "This is not a toy, Mr. Elephant. You must get out now and do your shopping. Look, here is the floorwalker."

30. Study for pp. 12–13.

Il entre dans un grand magasin. Il trouve l'ascenseur tellement drôle qu'il ne veut plus en sortir. Il monte 10 fois tout en haut. Il descend 10 fois tout en bas. A la fin le monsieur qui fait marcher l'ascenseur lui dit de sortir pour acheter ce qu'il veut acheter. [Written upside down:] n'est pas 1 joujou

He goes into a big store. He thinks the elevator is so much fun that he never wants to get out. He goes all the way up 10 times. He goes all the way down 10 times. Finally the man who runs the elevator tells him to get out and do his shopping. *[Written upside down:]* This is not a toy.

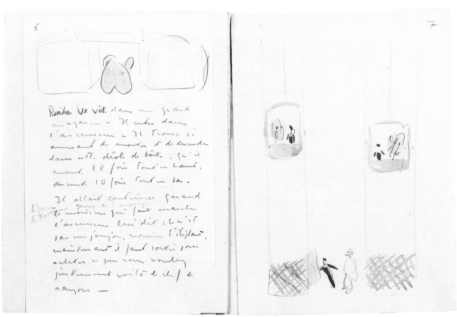

29

30

Shopping Spree

31. Dummy for pp. 14–15.
Alors il s'achète: une chemise avec col et cravate, un costume d'une agréable couleur verte, puis un beau chapeau melon, enfin des souliers avec des guêtres.

Then he buys himself: a shirt with a collar and tie, a suit of a becoming shade of green, then a handsome derby hat, and finally shoes with spats.

32. Maquette, pp. 8–9 (corresponding to pp. 14–15 of published book).
Alors il s'achète une belle chemise avec col et cravate et un beau chapeau. / Puis un beau costume. Enfin de belles chaussures avec guêtres.

Then he buys himself a beautiful shirt with a collar and tie and a beautiful hat. / Then a beautiful suit, and finally some beautiful shoes with spats.

33. Study for pp. 14–15.
Il s'achète une bell[e] chem[ise], un beau costume, un beau chapeau, et des chaussures / beaux souliers.

He buys himself a beautiful shirt, a beautiful suit, a beautiful hat, and some shoes / beautiful shoes.

34. Study for pp. 14–15.
Il s'achète une belle chemise avec col et cravate, un beau costume, un beau chapeau, et des beaux souliers.

He buys himself a beautiful shirt with a collar and tie, a beautiful suit, a beautiful hat, and some beautiful shoes.

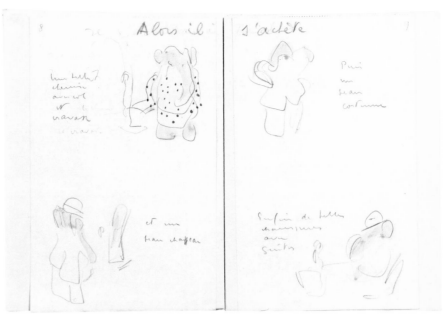

32

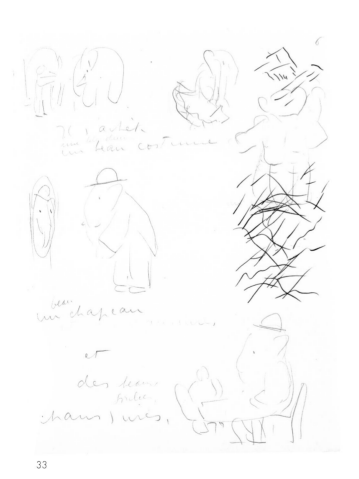

33

34

The Photographer

très content
de ses achats
et satisfait
de son élégance,
Babar va
chez le photographe.

_16_

HISTOIRE DE BABAR
Jean de Brunhoff.

35

Et voilà sa photographie.

_17_

36

35. Dummy for p. 16.
Très content de ses achats et satisfait de son élégance, Babar va chez le photographe.

Well satisfied with his purchases and feeling very elegant indeed, Babar goes to the photographer's studio.

36. Dummy for p. 17.
Et voilà sa photographie.

And here is his photograph.

37. Maquette, pp. 10–11 (corresponding to pp. 16–17 of published book).
Très content de ses achats et satisfait de son élégance Babar va se faire photographier. / Photo de Babar

Well satisfied with his purchases and feeling very elegant indeed, Babar goes to have his photograph taken. / Photo of Babar

38. Study for p. 16.
En sortant du magasin il se trouve si beau qu'il va chez un photographe pour se faire photographier.

After he leaves the store he thinks he looks so good that he goes to a photographer's studio to have his photograph taken.

Babar
va se faire
photographier

Photo de Babar

37

En sortant du
magasin il se
trouve si beau
qu'il va chez
un photografe
tous se faire
Photographier

Life with the Old Lady

39

40

39. First edition, p. 18.

Babar va dîner chez son amie la vieille dame. Elle le trouve très chic dans son costume neuf. Après le dîner, fatigué, il s'endort vite.

Babar dines with his friend the Old Lady. She thinks he looks very smart in his new clothes. After dinner, feeling tired, he falls asleep quickly.

40. Dummy for p. 19.

Maintenant Babar habite chez la vieille dame. Le matin, avec elle, il fait de la gymnastique, puis il prend son bain.

Babar now lives at the Old Lady's house. In the mornings, he does exercises with her, and then he takes his bath.

41. Maquette, pp. 12–13 (corresponding to pp. 18–19 of published book).

Babar va dîner chez son amie la vieille dame. Elle le trouve vraiment très chic dans son costume neuf. Après dîner, fatigué, il s'endort vite. / Maintenant Babar habite chez la vieille dame. Le matin il fait de la gymnastique avec elle et après prend son bain. Il se douche avec sa trompe.

Babar dines with his friend, the Old Lady. She thinks he looks very smart in his new clothes. After dinner, feeling tired, he falls asleep quickly. / Babar now lives at the Old Lady's house. In the mornings he does exercises with her and then takes his bath. He showers with his trunk.

42. Study for p. 18.

En sortant de chez le photographe, il va dîner chez la vieille dame qui lui avait donné le porte-monnaie et qui l'avait invité. La vieille dame le trouve si très joli et bien habillé! Mais Bébé éléphant après cette journée fatiguante [i.e., fatigante] est a bien sommeil. Le voilà qui dort dans le lit que la vieille dame lui a préparé.

After leaving the photographer's studio, he dines with the Old Lady who had given him her purse and who had invited him over. The Old Lady thinks he looks so very nice and very well dressed! But after this exhausting day Baby Elephant is very tired. Here he is sleeping in the bed that the Old Lady has prepared for him.

41

42

Automobile Ride

43. Dummy for pp. 20–21.

Tous les jours il se promène en auto. C'est la vieille dame qui la lui a achetée. Elle lui donne tout ce qu'il veut.

He goes out for an automobile ride every day. The Old Lady has bought him the car. She gives him whatever he wants.

44. Maquette, p. 15 (corresponding to pp. 20–21 of published book).

Tous les jours il se promène dans l'auto que la vieille dame lui a acheté[e]. La vieille dame lui donne tout ce qu'il veut.

Every day he goes for a ride in the car the Old Lady has bought for him. The Old Lady gives him whatever he wants.

45. Study for pp. 20–21.

La vieille dame le voyant triste, lui achète une automobile pour— Le voilà Bébé El. est très content pendant quelques jours il apprend à conduire son auto et pendant un mois il ne la quitte plus mais il n'oublie pas, il ne peut oublier la grande forêt où il est né.

Seeing how sad he is, the Old Lady buys him a car to— Here he is Baby El. is very happy for a few days he learns to drive his car and for a month he is never away from it but he never forgets, he cannot forget the great forest where he was born.

46. Study for pp. 20–21.

Tous les jours il se promène dans l'auto que la vieille dame lui a acheté[e]. La vieille dame lui donne tout ce qu'il veut.

Every day he goes for a ride in the car that the Old Lady has bought for him. The Old Lady gives him whatever he wants.

44

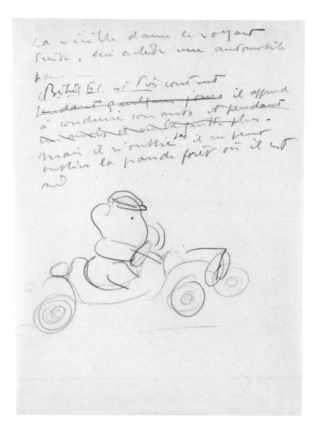

45

46

The Educated Elephant

Un savant professeur lui donne des leçons.
Babar fait attention
et répond comme il faut.
C'est un élève qui fait des progrès.

-22-

Le soir, après dîner, il raconte
aux amis de la vieille dame
sa vie dans la grande forêt..

47. Dummy for p. 22.
Un savant professeur lui donne des leçons. Babar fait attention et répond comme il faut. C'est un élève qui fait des progrès.

A learned professor gives him lessons. Babar pays attention and answers appropriately. He is a student who makes progress.

48. First edition, p. 23.
Le soir, après dîner, il raconte aux amis de la vieille dame sa vie dans la grande forêt.

In the evening, after dinner, he tells the Old Lady's friends all about his life in the great forest.

49. Study for p. 22.
Un excellent professeur lui donne des leçons. Babar fait attention et répond comme il faut. C'est un élève qui fait des progrès.

An accomplished professor gives him lessons. Babar pays attention and answers appropriately. He is a student who makes progress.

50. Maquette, p. 14 (corresponding to p. 23 of published book).
Le soir après dîner, il raconte aux amis de la vieille dame sa vie dans la grande forêt.

In the evening, after dinner, he tells the Old Lady's friends all about his life in the great forest.

51. Study for p. 23.
Bébé éléphant resta chez la vieille dame. Le soir après dîner il racontait aux amis de la vieille dame sa vie dans la grande forêt avec sa maman et ses ~~amis, et les amis de la vieille dame [also deleted: l']écoutaient ses histoires sans se lasser~~

Baby Elephant stayed with the Old Lady. In the evening, after dinner, he would tell the Old Lady's friends about his life in the great forest with his mother and his ~~friends, and the Old Lady's friends listened to his stories tirelessly~~

22

*Un excellent professeur lui donne
des leçons — Babar fait attention
et répond comme il faut
C'est un élève qui fait des progrès*

49

14

*Le soir après dîner,
il raconte aux amis de la
vieille dame sa vie dans la
grande forêt —*

50

*Babar l'éléphant resta chez la
vieille dame — Le soir après dîner
il racontait sa vie dans la
grande forêt avec sa maman
et ses amis aux amis de la
vieille dame*

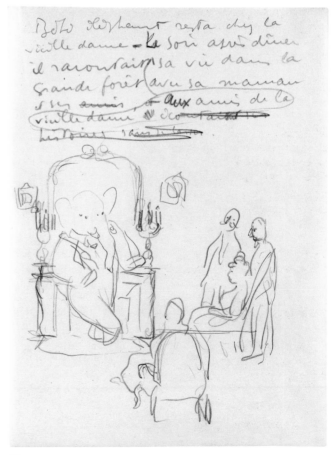

51

Remembering *Maman*

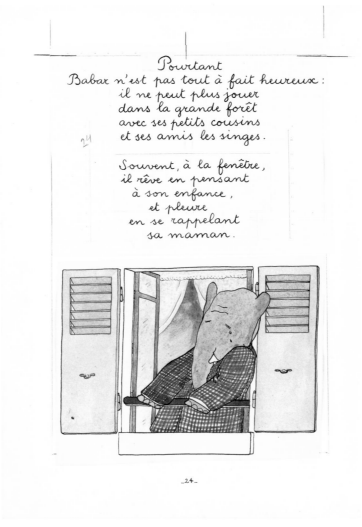

52

52. Dummy for p. 24.
Pourtant Babar n'est pas tout à fait heureux: il ne peut plus jouer dans la grande forêt avec ses petits cousins et ses amis les singes. Souvent, à la fenêtre, il rêve en pensant à son enfance, et pleure en se rappelant sa maman.

And yet Babar is not entirely happy, for he can no longer play in the great forest with his little cousins and his friends, the monkeys. He often stands at the window, thinking of his childhood, and cries when he remembers his mother.

53. Maquette, p. 16 (corresponding to p. 24 of published book).
Pourtant Babar n'est pas t[ou]t à fait heureux: il ne peut plus jouer dans la grande forêt avec ses petits cousins et ses amis les singes. Souvent à la fenêtre il rêve en pensant à la grande forêt et pleure en se rappelant sa maman.

And yet Babar is not entirely happy: he can no longer play in the great forest with his little cousins and his friends, the monkeys. He often stands at the window thinking about the great forest, and he cries when he remembers his mother.

54. Study for p. 24.
Bébé éléphant avait tout ce qu'il voulait chez la vieille dame et pourtant il n'était pas tout à fait heureux, ~~juste ment~~ parce que ~~la grande forêt~~ il ne pouvait plus jouer dans la grande forêt avec ses petits cousins et ses amis les singes. ~~Souvent il rêvait~~ Le voilà à la fenêtre qui rêve pensant à la grande forêt et pleurant en se rappelant sa maman.

Baby Elephant had everything he wanted at the Old Lady's house, and yet he was not entirely happy, because ~~the great forest~~ he could no longer play in the great forest with his little cousins and his friends, the monkeys. ~~He often thought~~ Here he is at the window, thinking about the great forest and crying when he remembers his mother.

16

Pourtant Babar n'est pas
Il a fait heureux : il ne peut
plus jouer dans la grande forêt
avec ses petits cousins et ses amis
les singes — Souvent à la fenêtre
il rêve en pensant à la grande
forêt et pleure en se rappelant
sa maman

53

Babar éléphant avait tout ce
qu'il voulait chez la vieille dame
et pourtant il n'était pas tout
à fait heureux, ~~justement~~ #
~~car~~ parce que la grande forêt il ne
pourrait plus jouer dans la
grande forêt avec ses petits cousins
et les amis les singes ~~souvent~~ pensant
~~le voilà à la fenêtre souvent rêvait~~ à la grande
~~souvent~~ il rêvait à la grande
forêt et pleurait en se rappelant
sa maman ———

54

71

Arthur and Celeste

55

56

55. First edition, p. 25.

Deux années ont passé. Un jour pendant sa promenade il voit venir à sa rencontre deux petits éléphants tout nus. « Mais c'est Arthur et Céleste, mon petit cousin et ma cousine! » dit-il stupéfait à la vieille dame.

Two years have passed. One day during his walk he sees two little elephants, completely naked, coming toward him. "Why," he says in astonishment to the Old Lady, "it's Arthur and Celeste, my little cousins!"

56. Maquette, p. 17 (not included in published book but related to p. 25).

Pendant ce temps 2 petits éléphants se sauvent loin de la forêt et courent de toutes leurs forces.

Meanwhile 2 little elephants escape faraway from the forest, running as fast as they can.

57. Maquette, p. 18 (corresponding to p. 25 of published book).

Et un beau jour, pendant la promenade avec la vieille dame, Babar voit venir à sa rencontre 2 petits éléphants tout nus.

And one fine day, during his walk with the Old Lady, Babar sees 2 little elephants, completely naked, coming toward him.

58. Study for p. 25.

Un jour il se promenait comme d'habitude avec la vieille dame, quand tout à coup tout étonné il aperçut venant à sa rencontre deux petits éléphants tout nus—et il reconnut ses deux petits cousins Arthur et Céleste.

One day he was taking his usual walk with the Old Lady when all of a sudden he was astonished to see two little elephants, completely naked, coming toward him—and he recognized his two little cousins, Arthur and Celeste.

59. Study for p. 25.

Babar reste tout de même chez la vieille dame parce qu'il l'aime bien, et voilà qu'un beau jour pendant sa promenade il voit venir à sa rencontre deux petits éléphants tout nus.

All the same, Babar stays with the Old Lady because he is fond of her, and one fine day during his walk he sees two little elephants, completely naked, coming toward him.

60. Draft of text for p. 25.

Néanmoins B. reste / Le temps passe et B. est t[ou]j[ou]rs chez son amie la v.d. / son amie / Babar reste chez la v.d. / Un an après Babar est encore chez la v.d. son amie / Pendant un an B. reste chez la v.d. / un jour il se promène pendant sa promenade il voit venir à sa rencontre deux petits él. tout nus. / 25 / Le temps passe / Babar est toujours chez son amie la vieille dame / un jour pendant sa promenade il voit venir à sa rencontre deux petits éléphants tout nus. « Mais c'est Arthur et Céleste » dit il stupéfait Babar à la vieille dame.

Nevertheless B. stays / Time passes and B. is still with the O.L. / his friend / Babar stays with the O.L. / A year later Babar is still staying with his friend the O.L. / For a year B. has been staying with the O.L. / one day he is walking during his walk he sees two little el., completely naked, coming toward him / 25 / Time passes / Babar is still at his friend the Old Lady's place / one day during his walk he sees two little elephants, completely naked, coming toward him. "Well, if it isn't Arthur and Celeste, " he says, astonished says Babar to the Old Lady.

57

58

59

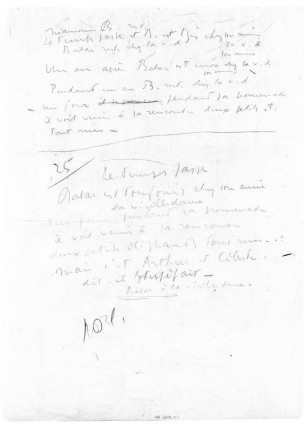

60

Cousins in the City

61

61. Dummy for p. 26.
Babar embrasse Arthur et Céleste puis il va leur acheter de beaux costumes.

Babar kisses Arthur and Celeste and goes to buy them some fine clothes.

62. Maquette, p. 19 (corresponding to upper portion of p. 26 of published book).
Babar reconnaît alors ses cousins Arthur et Céleste. Ils s'embrassent tous bien heureux. Arthur et Céleste s'étaient sauvés pour chercher Babar parce qu'ils avaient trop de chagrin depuis qu'il était parti et qu'ils avaient trop envie de jouer avec lui de nouveau.

Babar then recognizes his cousins Arthur and Celeste. They kiss each other joyously. Arthur and Celeste had run away to look for Babar because they were upset after he had left, and they wanted very much to play with him once again.

63. Maquette, p. 20 (corresponding to p. 26 of published book).
Vite Babar emmène Arthur et Céleste dans le grand magasin et leur achète de beaux costumes.

Babar hurries to take Arthur and Celeste to the big store and buys them some fine clothes.

64. Study for p. 26.
Bébé éléphant qui avait encore un peu d'argent vite les emmène dans le grand magasin pour leur acheter aussi de beaux costumes. Les voilà habillés avec leur costume neuf.

Baby Elephant, who still had a bit of money, quickly takes them to the big store to buy them some fine clothes as well. Here they are dressed in their new outfits.

65. Study for p. 26.
Après s'être embrassés, les petits cousins lui racontèrent qu'ils s'étaient sauvés loin de la forêt pour le chercher, parce qu'ils avaient trop de chagrin depuis qu'il était parti et qu'ils avaient trop envie de jouer de nouveau avec lui.

After they all kissed, the little cousins told him that they had run faraway from the forest to look for him because they were very upset after he had left and they very much wanted to play with him once again.

66. Study for p. 26.
Il reconnaît bientôt/alors son cousin Arthur et sa cousine Céleste. Tous trois s'embrassent bien heureux. Arthur et Céleste s'étaient sauvés de la

62

63

forêt pour retrouver Babar parce qu'ils avaient trop envie de le revoir et de jouer avec lui.

He soon/then recognizes his cousins Arthur and Celeste. All three embrace joyfully. Arthur and Celeste had run away from the forest to find Babar because they were so eager to see him again and to play with him.

67. Study for p. 26.
vite des habits [remainder of text torn away]

some clothes quickly

Bébé l'Eléphant qui avait
eu ... un peu d'argent
vite
les emmène
dans le grand
magasin

AUX GALERIES

pour leur acheter
aussi de beaux costumes

les voilà habillés avec leur costume neuf.

64

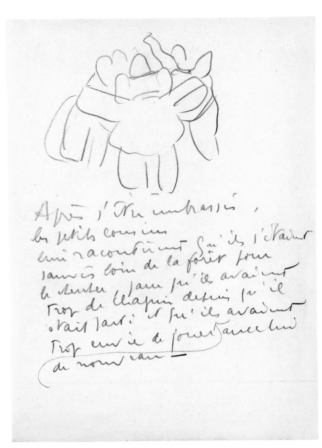

Après s'être embrassés,
les petits cousins
lui racontèrent qu'ils s'étaient
sauvés loin de la forêt pour
le chercher parce qu'il avait
trop de chagrin depuis qu'il
était parti et qu'ils avaient
trop envie de pouvoir ...lui
de nouveau

65

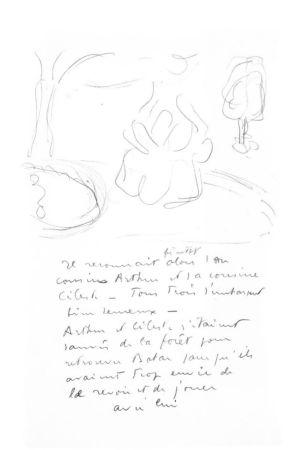

Il reconnait alors son
cousins Arthur et la cousine
Céleste — Tous trois s'embrassent
bien tendrement —
Arthur et Céleste s'étaient
sauvés de la forêt pour
retrouver Babar parce qu'ils
avaient trop envie de
le revoir et de jouer
avec lui

66

67

Eclairs All Around

69

68. First edition, p. 27.
Il les emmène chez le pâtissier manger de bons gâteaux.

He takes them to a pastry shop to eat some delicious cakes.

69. Maquette, p. 21 (corresponding to p. 27 of published book).
Maintenant Babar ~~leur montre~~ les promène dans la ville et les mène chez le pâtissier.

Then Babar ~~shows them~~ takes them into town and into the pastry shop.

70. Study for p. 27.
Après s'être embrassé[s] ils allèrent tous manger de bons gâteaux chez le pâtissier ~~et décidèrent de repartir tous dans la grande forêt, où tout le monde serait bien content de les revoir.~~

They kissed each other and then set off to eat delicious cakes at the pastry shop ~~and they all decided to go back to the great forest, where everyone would be happy to see them again.~~

71. Study for p. 27.
Après Bébé E leur montre les beautés de la ville, et les mène chez le pâtissier.

Then Baby E shows them the delights of the town and leads them into the pastry shop.

72. Study for p. 27.

73. Study for p. 27.

70

71

72

73

A Frantic Search

74. Dummy for pp. 28–29.
Pendant ce temps dans la forêt, les éléphants cherchent et appellent Arthur et Céleste, et leurs mamans sont bien inquiètes. Heureusement, en volant sur la ville, un vieux marabout les a vus. Vite il vient prévenir les éléphants.

Meanwhile, in the forest, the elephants are calling and hunting for Arthur and Celeste, and their mothers are very worried. Fortunately, in flying over the town, an old marabou has seen them. He comes back quickly to tell the elephants.

75. Maquette, pp. 22–23 (corresponding to pp. 28–29 of published book).
Pendant ce temps, bien inquiètes, les mamans de Céleste et d'Arthur les cherchent partout [et] les appellent. / A force de courir en appelant [i.e., appelant] « Arthur, Céleste » les mamans rencontrent la girafe. La girafe leur dit avoir vu passer Babar il y a longtemps et qu'il courait vers la ville. Peut-être Arthur et Céleste l'ont-ils rejoint?

Meanwhile, Celeste's and Arthur's mothers, feeling very worried, search everywhere for them, calling out their names. / After running and calling "Arthur, Celeste" for awhile, the mothers run into the giraffe. The giraffe tells them that he saw Babar go by a long time ago and that he was running toward town. Perhaps Arthur and Celeste have met up with him?

76. Study for p. 29.
~~Mais~~ Pendant ce temps les mamans ~~éléphants~~ des petits cousins éléphants ne trouvent plus ~~les petits cousins éléphants~~ leurs enfants dans la forêt. Elles les appellent: et les cherchent partout.

~~But~~ Meanwhile the little elephant cousins' mothers cannot find ~~the little elephant cousins~~ their children in the forest. They call out their names: and look everywhere for them.

77. Study for p. 29.
~~Elles~~ A force de courir en appelant [i.e., appelant] leurs petits les mamans éléphants rencontrent la girafe qui leur dit avoir vu passer Bébé éléphant et plus tard les petits cousins et que tous allaient vers la ville.

~~They~~ After running and calling their little ones for awhile, the mother elephants meet the giraffe, who tells them that he has seen Baby Elephant, and later the little cousins, go by and that they were all heading toward town.

78. Study for pp. 28–29.
Pendant ce temps dans la forêt tous les éléphants cherchent et appellent Arthur et Céleste. Les mamans d'Arthur et Céleste sont bien inquiètes. Heureusement la girafe leur donne le conseil d'aller à la ville, peut-être ont ils rejoint Babar.

Meanwhile in the forest all the elephants look for Arthur and Celeste and call their names. The mothers of Arthur and Celeste are very worried. Fortunately the giraffe advises them to go to town; perhaps they have met up with Babar.

75

76

77

78

79

Angry Aunts

79

80

79. Dummy for p. 30.

Les mamans d'Arthur et de Céleste sont venues les chercher à la ville. Elles sont bien contentes de les retrouver, mais elles les grondent tout de même parce qu'ils se sont sauvés.

The mothers of Arthur and Celeste have come to the town fetch them. They are very happy to have them back, but they scold them just the same because they ran away.

80. Dummy for p. 31.

Babar se décide à partir avec Arthur, Céleste et leurs mamans, et à revoir la grande forêt. Aidé par la vieille dame, il fait sa malle.

Babar makes up his mind to go back with Arthur and Celeste and their mothers to see the great forest again. The Old Lady helps him to pack his trunk.

81. Maquette, pp. 24–25 (corresponding to p. 30 of published book).

Les mamans ont retrouvé Céleste, Arthur, et Babar. Elles sont bien contentes, mais elles le gronde[nt] tout de même. / Elles leur disent que demain, pas plus tard, elles les remmèneront dans la grande forêt. Si Babar n'était pas triste de laisser la vie[ille] son amie la vieille dame, il serait très content de partir.

The mothers have found Celeste, Arthur, and Babar. They are very happy but scold them just the same. / They tell them that tomorrow, no later, they will take them back to the great forest. If Babar were not sad about leaving the O[ld] his friend, the Old Lady, he would be very glad to be going.

82. Study for pp. 30–31.

Les mamans sont arrivées à la ville. Elles retrouvent Arthur et Céleste. Elles sont bien contentes mais elles les gronde[nt] tout de même parce qu'ils se sont sauvés. Elles vont repartir à la forêt avec Arthur et Céleste. Babar décide de partir aussi. S'il n'avait pas du chagrin de quitter la vieille dame il serait très content de faire ce voyage. Le voilà qui fait sa malle.

The mothers have arrived in town. They find Arthur and Celeste. They are very happy, but they scold them just the same for running away. They are going to return to the forest with Arthur and Celeste. Babar decides to leave as well. If he were not upset about leaving the Old Lady, he would be very happy to make this trip. Here he is packing his trunk.

83. Draft of text for pp. 20–21 and 30.

La vieille dame le voyant triste lui achète une auto / les petits cousins / les mamans / comment peux tu vivre chez les hommes / Oublies-tu que ta mère a été tuée—

Seeing how sad he is, the Old Lady buys him a car / the little cousins / the mothers / how can you live among men / Have you forgotten that your mother was killed—

81

82

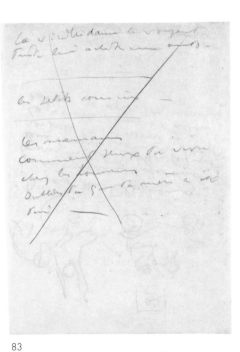

83

Farewell, Friend

85

84. Dummy for p. 32.

Tout est prêt pour le départ. Babar embrasse sa vieille amie. S'il n'avait pas le chagrin de la laisser, il serait tout à fait heureux de partir. Il lui promet de revenir. Jamais il ne l'oubliera.

Everything is ready for their departure. Babar kisses his old friend. He would be quite happy to go if it were not for leaving her. He promises to come back some day. He will never forget her.

85. Study for p. 32.

Les mamans éléphants et les petits cousins Il Bébé Eléphant va dire au revoir à la vieille dame, l'embrasse et lui donne sa photographe [i.e., photographie] avec sa signature.

The mother elephants and the little cousins He Baby Elephant goes to say good-bye to the Old Lady, kisses her and gives her his signed photograph.

86. Maquette, pp. 26–27 (corresponding to pp. 32–33 of published book).

Babar va dire au revoir à la vieille dame, l'embrasse et lui donne sa photo avec sa signature. / Babar fait sa malle. La vieille dame lui apporte des gâteaux pour le voyage et l'aide à fermer sa malle. Elle est très triste.

Babar goes to say good-bye to the Old Lady, kisses her, and gives her his signed photograph. / Babar packs his trunk. The Old Lady brings him some cookies for the trip and helps him close his trunk. She is very sad.

87. Study for pp. 32–33.

N'ayant plus faire ils partent tous les cinq dans une auto pour ils décident veulent Maintenant ils ont tous envie de retourner dans la grande forêt et pour y arriver/aller plus vite ils achètent une belle auto rouge Torpédo. Les voilà qui partent après avoir acheté pris un paquet de gâteaux pour la route le voyage. Sur son balcon la vieille dame leur dit au revoir en agitant son mouchoir.

With nothing more to do, all five of them leave in a car to They decide They want Now they all want to return to the great forest, and in order to get there more quickly they buy a beautiful red car Torpedo. Here they are going on their way after buying getting a box of cookies for the road their trip. The Old Lady says good-bye to them from her balcony, waving her handkerchief.

88. Study for p. 33.

Départ des Eléphants. Les mamans préfèrent courir derrière. Elles lèvent leur trompe pour ne pas respirer la poussière. La vieille dame est à son balcon et agite son mouchoir.

The elephants' departure. The mothers prefer to run along behind. They lift up their trunks to avoid breathing in the dust. The Old Lady is on her balcony waving her handkerchief.

86

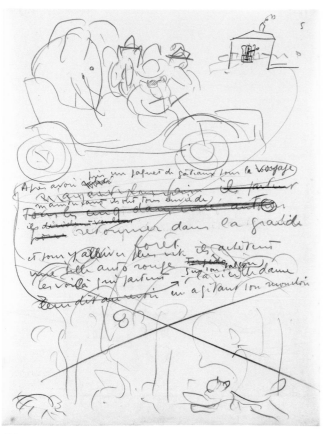

87

88

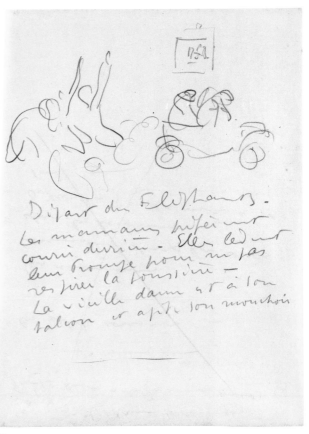

The Old Lady, Alone

90

89. Dummy for p. 33.

Ils sont partis. . . . Les mamans n'ont pas de place dans l'auto, elles courent derrière et lèvent leurs trompes pour ne pas respirer la poussière. La vieille dame reste seule; triste, elle pense: « Quand reverrai-je mon petit Babar? »

They have gone. . . . There is no room in the car for the mothers, so they run behind, and lift up their trunks to avoid breathing the dust. The Old Lady is left alone. Sadly she wonders: "When shall I see my little Babar again?"

90. Maquette, p. 28 (corresponding to p. 33 of published book).

Babar part pour la forêt. Les mamans préfèrent courir derrière l'auto. Elles lèvent leur trompe pour ne pas respirer la poussière. La vieille dame est à son balcon.

Babar sets out for the forest. The mothers prefer to run behind the car. They lift up their trunks to avoid breathing in the dust. The Old Lady is on her balcony.

91. Study for p. 33.

Babar est parti en auto avec Arthur et Céleste. Les mamans suivent derrière. Elles lèvent leur trompe pour ne pas avaler la poussière. [La] vieille [dame] est à son balcon [text torn away] reste toute seule. Elle est très triste.

Babar has left in the car with Arthur and Celeste. The mothers follow behind. They lift up their trunks to avoid swallowing the dust. [The] Old [Lady] is on her balcony [text torn away] is now all alone. She is very sad.

92. Study for pp. 32–33.

93. Study for pp. 32–33.

Tout est prêt pour le départ. Babar embrasse une dernière fois sa vieille amie, s'il n'avait pas le chagrin de la laisser il serait tout à fait heureux de partir. Il lui promet de revenir. / Ils sont partis. La vieille dame reste seule [et] ne peut se consoler. Elle est terriblement triste.

Everything is ready for their departure. Babar kisses his old friend one last time; if he were not upset about leaving her he would be quite happy to leave. He promises her that he will return. / They have left. The Old Lady is now alone [and] inconsolable. She is terribly sad.

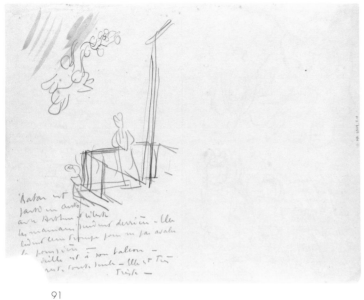

91

92

93

A Bad Mushroom

94. First edition, p. 34.

Le même jour hélas, le roi des éléphants a mangé un mauvais champignon.

Alas, that very day, the king of the elephants has eaten a bad mushroom.

95. Dummy for p. 35.

Empoisonné, il a été très malade, si malade qu'il en est mort. C'est un grand malheur. / Après l'enterrement les plus vieux des éléphants se sont réunis pour choisir un nouveau roi.

It poisoned him, and he became ill, so ill that he died. This was a great calamity. / After the funeral the oldest elephants held a meeting to choose a new king.

96. Study for p. 34.

97. Study for p. 34.

98. Maquette, p. 29 (corresponding to p. 35 of published book).

Pendant ce temps le vieux Roi des éléphants est mort après une longue maladie. Il n'a pas d'enfant et les plus vieux des éléphants cherchent un nouveau Roi.

Meanwhile, the old elephant king died after a long illness. He does not have children, so the oldest elephants are looking for a new king.

99. Study for p. 35.

Le vieux roi des Eléphants était mort il y avait peu de temps, les plus âgés des éléphants décidèrent de nommer roi à sa place Bébé éléphant.

The old king of the elephants had died a short while ago; the oldest elephants decided to appoint Baby Elephant as king in his place.

96

97

Pendant ce temps le vieux
Roi des éléphants est mort
après une longue maladie
il n'a pas d'enfants et
les plus vieux des éléphants
cherchent un nouveau
Roi —

29

98

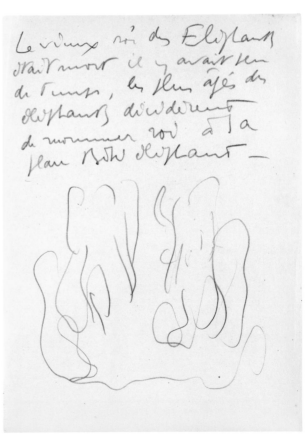

Le vieux roi des Eléphants
était mort il y avait peu
de temps, les plus âgés des
éléphants décidèrent
de nommer roi à la
place notre éléphant —

99

Triumphant Return

100. Dummy for pp. 36–37.

Juste à ce moment ils entendent du bruit, ils se retournent. Qu'est-ce qu'ils voient! Babar qui arrive dans son auto et tous les éléphants qui courent en criant: « Les voilà! Les voilà! Ils sont revenus! Bonjour Babar! Bonjour Arthur! Bonjour Céleste! Quels beaux costumes! Quelle belle auto! »

Just then they hear a noise. They turn around. Guess what they see! Babar arriving in his car and all the elephants running and shouting: "Here they are! Here they are! They have returned! Hello, Babar! Hello, Arthur! Hello, Celeste! What beautiful clothes! What a beautiful car!"

101. Maquette, pp. 30–31 (corresponding to pp. 36–37 of published book).

C'est alors que Babar arrive dans la grande forêt avec son auto, Céleste et Arthur. Tous les éléphants les trouve[nt] si beaux avec leurs beaux costumes et leur auto qu'ils crient tous: « Bravo / Bravo / Vive Arthur / Vive Babar / Vive Céleste / Qu'ils sont beaux / Vive le Roi »

Just then Babar arrives in the great forest with his car, Celeste, and Arthur. All the elephants think they look so nice in their fine clothes and their car that they all shout: "Bravo / Bravo / Long live Arthur / Long live Babar / Long live Celeste / Don't they look wonderful / Long live the king"

102. Study for p. 37.

Arrivés dans la forêt / Tous les éléphants les trouvent tellement beaux dans leurs beaux costumes et leur belle auto qu'ils décident de les faire tout de suite rois tous les trois. « Bravo / Vive le Roy [i.e., Roi] / Bébé Roi / Oh qu'ils sont beaux »

Arrived in the forest / All the elephants think they look so nice in their fine clothes and their beautiful car that they decide to appoint all three of them king right away. "Bravo / Long live the King / Baby King / Oh don't they look wonderful"

101

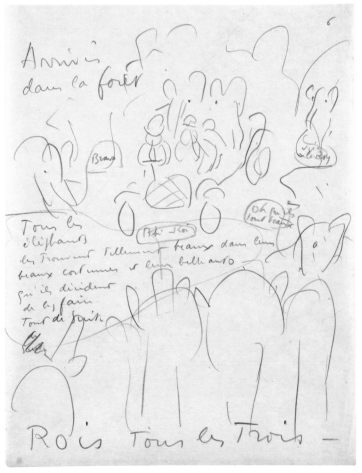

102

Alors Cornélius
le plus vieux des éléphants
dit de sa voix tremblante :
« Mes bons amis, nous cherchons un roi,
pourquoi ne pas choisir Babar ?
Il revient de la ville,
il a beaucoup appris chez les hommes.
Donnons lui la couronne. »
Tous les éléphants trouvent
que Cornélius a très bien parlé.
Impatients,
ils attendent la réponse de Babar.

« Je vous remercie tous,
dit alors ce dernier,
mais avant d'accepter,
je dois vous dire
que, pendant notre voyage en auto,
Céleste et moi
nous nous sommes fiancés.
Si je suis votre roi, elle sera votre reine. »

Vive la reine Céleste !

Vive le roi Babar !!!
crient tous les éléphants sans hésiter.
Et c'est ainsi que Babar devint roi.

IEF·6

-38-

-39-

103   104

103. Dummy for p. 38.
Alors Cornélius le plus vieux des éléphants dit de sa voix tremblante: « Mes bons amis, nous cherchons un roi, pourquoi ne pas choisir Babar? Il revient de la ville, il a beaucoup appris chez les hommes. Donnons lui la couronne. » Tous les éléphants trouvent que Cornélius a très bien parlé. Impatients, ils attendent la réponse de Babar. / « Je vous remercie tous, dit alors ce dernier, mais avant d'accepter, je dois vous dire que, pendant notre voyage en auto, Céleste et moi nous nous sommes fiancés. Si je suis votre roi, elle sera votre reine. » / « Vive la reine Céleste! / Vive le roi Babar!!! » crient tous les éléphants sans hésiter. Et c'est ainsi que Babar devint roi.

Then Cornelius, the oldest of all the elephants, says in his quavering voice: "My good friends, we are seeking a king. Why not choose Babar? He has just returned from the city, he has learned so much living among men, let us give him the crown." All the other elephants think that Cornelius has spoken wisely, and

they eagerly await Babar's reply. / "I want to thank you one and all," said Babar, "but before accepting your proposal, I must explain to you that, while we were traveling in the car, Celeste and I became engaged. If I become your king, she will be your queen." / "Long live Queen Celeste! Long live King Babar!!!" cry all the elephants without a moment's hesitation. And thus it was that Babar became king.

104. Dummy for p. 39.

105. Maquette, pp. 32–33 (corresponding to pp. 38–39 of published book).
« Voilà le roi que nous cherchions » dire[nt] les plus vieux des éléphants. Le plus vieux de tous dit à Babar « Voulez vous être notre Roi? » « Je veux bien, dit Babar, mais je veux aussi que Céleste soit ma femme et votre reine. » « Vive Babar I Vive Céleste » crièrent tous les éléphants. / Quelques jours après Babar envoye [i.e., envoie] à tous les animaux cette invitation: « Nous Babar I, roi des éléphants, vous invitons à venir assister à notre mariage avec notre cousine Céleste et aux fêtes de notre couronnement. »

"Here is the king we have been searching for," say the oldest elephants. The oldest one of all says to Babar, "Would you like to be our King?" "I would like that very much," says Babar, "but I would also like Celeste to be my wife and your queen." "Long live Babar I, Long live Celeste," all the elephants shouted. / A few days later Babar sends this invitation to all the animals: "We, Babar I, king of the elephants, invite you to attend our marriage to our cousin Celeste and our coronation festivities."

106. Study for p. 39.

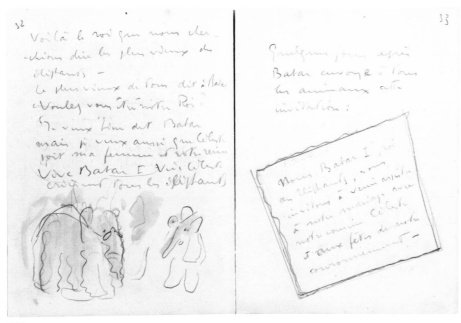

105

106

Wedding Plans

107. Dummy for p. 40.
Babar dit à Cornélius: « Tu as de bonnes idées, aussi je te nomme général, et quand j'aurai la couronne je te donnerai mon chapeau. Dans huit jours j'épouserai Céleste. Nous aurons alors une grande fête pour notre mariage et notre couronnement. » Ensuite Babar demande aux oiseaux d'aller inviter tous les animaux,

"You have good ideas," says Babar to Cornelius. "I will therefore make you a general, and when I get my crown, I will give you my hat. In eight days I shall marry Celeste. We will then have a splendid party in honor of our marriage and our coronation." Then, turning to the birds, Babar asks them to go and invite all the animals to the festivities,

108. First edition, p. 41.
et charge le dromadaire de lui acheter à la ville de beaux habits de noce.

and he tells the dromedary to go to the town and buy him some beautiful wedding clothes.

109. Dummy for p. 42.
Les invités commencent à arriver. Le dromadaire rapporte les costumes juste à temps pour le mariage.

The wedding guests begin to arrive. The dromedary returns with the bridal costumes just in the nick of time for the ceremony.

110. Maquette, pp. 34–35 (corresponding to pp. 42 and 44–45 of published book).
Tous les animaux viennent au mariage et au couronnement de Babar et de Céleste.

All the animals come to the marriage and coronation of Babar and Celeste.

Les invités commencent à arriver. 42
Le dromadaire rapporte les costumes
juste à temps pour le mariage.

_42_

109

110

A Royal Wedding

112

111. Dummy for p. 43.

112. Study for p. 43.
A son couronnement vinrent tous les animaux.

All the animals came to his coronation.

113. Study for p. 43.
C'est ainsi que Bébé Eléphant et ses 2 petits cousins éléphants sont devenus Rois des Eléphants.

That is how Baby Elephant and his 2 little elephant cousins became Kings of the Elephants.

114. Study for p. 43.
Le roi B[abar] épouse la r[eine] C[éleste]. Cornélius vient de leur donner les couronnes.

King B[abar] marries Q[ueen] C[eleste]. Cornelius has just given them their crowns.

115. Study for p. 43.
Voici le mariage et le couronnement du Roi Babar et de la reine Céleste. Cornélius vient de donner les couronnes.

Here is the marriage and coronation of King Babar and Queen Celeste. Cornelius has just given them their crowns.

C'a l'aini Jean Buti Eliphant
et
les 2 petits cousins Cliphants
sont devenus

ROIS des ELiphants

113

114

Voici le mariage et le couronnement
du Roi Babar et de la reine Céleste
Cornélius vient de donner la couronne

115

Everyone Dances Joyfully

116. First edition, pp. 44–45.
Après le mariage et le couronnement, tout le monde danse de bon coeur.

After the wedding and the coronation everybody dances merrily.

117. Study for pp. 44–45.

118. Draft of text for pp. 44–45.
La grande fête organisée par Cornélius a un gros succès. Le bal surtout est réussi. On s'y amuse beaucoup et de bon coeur. / Après le mariage et le couronnement le grand bal a un gros succès est très réussi. Tout le monde danse de bon coeur, le lion comme la souris, Cornélius comme On s'amuse beaucoup et de bon coeur et longtemps chez les animaux on se rappellera cette belle fête.

The grand party organized by Cornelius is a huge success. The ball above all is successful. Everyone has a great and joyous time. / After the wedding and coronation the great ball is a huge success is very successful. Everyone dances joyfully, both the lion and the mouse, both Cornelius Everyone has a great and joyous time and for a long time the animals will remember this lovely party.

117

La grande fête organisée par Cornélius
a un gros succès –
Le bal surtout est réussi
On s'y amuse beaucoup et de bon
coeur –

Après le mariage et le couronnement
le grand bal ~~a un gros succès~~
Tout le monde danse de bon coeur,
le lion comme la souris,
~~Cornélius comme~~
On s'amuse beaucoup et de bon coeur
et longtemps chez les animaux on
se rappellera cette belle fête –

118

Reflection

La fête est finie,
la nuit est tombée,
les étoiles se sont levées.
Le roi Babar et la reine Céleste,
heureux,
rêvent à leur bonheur.

.46.

119

Maintenant tout dort,
les invités sont rentrés chez eux,
très contents mais fatigués
d'avoir trop dansé.
Longtemps
ils se rappelleront ce grand bal. __

.47.

120

119. Dummy for p. 46. (The illustration on this page is printed rather than drawn in ink, unlike all the other dummy illustrations.)
La fête est finie, la nuit est tombée, les étoiles se sont levées. Le roi Babar et la reine Céleste, heureux, rêvent à leur bonheur.

The festivities are over, night has fallen, the stars have risen in the sky. King Babar and Queen Celeste, feeling happy, reflect on their good fortune.

120. Dummy for p. 47.
Maintenant tout dort, les invités sont rentrés chez eux, très contents mais fatigués d'avoir trop dansé. Longtemps ils se rappelleront ce grand bal.

Now the world is asleep. The guests have gone home, happy, though tired from too much dancing. They will long remember this wonderful ball.

121. Variant dummy for p. 46.

122. Study for pp. 46–47.

La fête est finie,
la nuit est tombée,
les étoiles se sont levées,
le roi Babar et la reine Céleste,
heureux,
rêvent à leur bonheur....

121

122

Au Revoir!

123

123. Dummy for p. 48.
Dans un superbe ballon jaune, le roi Babar et la reine Céleste partent en voyage de noces pour de nouvelles aventures.

In a gorgeous yellow balloon, King Babar and Queen Celeste set out on their honeymoon for further adventures.

124. Maquette, p. 36 (corresponding to p. 46 of published book).
Le roi Babar I et la reine Céleste tels qu'ils étaient le jour de leur couronnement. Ici finit l'histoire de Babar le petit éléphant, mais vous pourrez savoir ce qu'il devient en lisant l'histoire du roi Babar.

King Babar I and Queen Celeste as they looked the day of their coronation. Here ends the story of Babar the little elephant, but you can find out what happens to him if you read the story of Babar the King.

125. Variant dummy for p. 48.
Babar, Arthur, et Céleste sont portés en triomphe par les éléphants. Ils vont maintenant se reposer. Dans un autre livre nous raconterons la suite de leurs aventures.

The elephants carried Babar, Arthur, and Celeste in triumph. They will now take a rest. In another book we will describe their continuing adventures.

36

Le roi Babar I et la reine Céleste
tels qu'ils étaient le jour de
leur couronnement —
ni finit l'histoire de Babar le
petit éléphant, mais vous pourrez
savoir ce qu'ils deviennent en lisant
l'histoire du roi Babar

124

36

Babar, Arthur et Céleste
sont portés en triomphe par les éléphants.
Ils vont maintenant se reposer.
Dans un autre livre nous raconterons
la suite de leurs aventures .—

125

Reproduced in this section are nearly all the surviving studies for Laurent de Brunhoff's first book, *Babar et ce coquin d'Arthur* (1946), along with the drawings used to print the first edition. The studies were generally executed in watercolor over graphite, while the final watercolors (the printer's dummy) are painted over black line proof. There are no surviving manuscript drafts for this book. The accompanying French text as well as the 1948 English translation by Merle Haas, lightly edited for this edition, have been provided.

Laurent de Brunhoff's
Babar et ce coquin d'Arthur

126

127

126. Study for cover.

127. Black line drawing for cover.

128. Dummy for title page.

129. Study for p. 3.

130. Dummy for p. 3.
Fatigués par une année de travail le roi Babar et la reine Céleste vont se reposer au bord de la mer avec leurs enfants. Arthur et Zéphir les accompagnent. Cornélius et la vieille dame ont fait quelques pas avec eux sur le chemin de la gare. « Au revoir! » crie Arthur. La vieille dame lui répond de loin.

Tired out by a year of hard work, King Babar and Queen Celeste start off with their children for a rest by the sea. Arthur and Zephir go along with them. Cornelius and the Old Lady walk partway to the station with them. "Au revoir!" Arthur cries. The Old Lady calls back from a distance.

128

129

130

Celesteville Train Station

131

132

133

131. Study for pp. 4–5.

132. Study for pp. 4–5.

133. Study for pp. 4–5.

134. Study for pp. 4–5.

135. Dummy for pp. 4–5.

Voici la gare de Célesteville. Tout joyeux d'être petits, Pom, Flore et Alexandre montent dans le train suspendu avec Zéphir. / Arthur voudrait bien en faire autant. « Voyons, lui dit Babar, tu es trop gros! Il faut venir avec les grandes personnes. »

Here is the Celesteville station. Pom, Flora, and Alexander, delighted at being young and small, climb aboard the overhead cable car with Zephir. / Arthur wishes he could go with them too. "But really," says Babar, "you are too fat! You must travel with the grown-ups."

134

135

A House in Baribarbotton

137

136. Study for p. 6.

137. Study for p. 7.

138. Study for pp. 7 and 10.

139. Dummy for pp. 6–7.
Pendant le voyage les trois petits éléphants regardent par le fenêtre; Arthur leur fait des signes. C'est très amusant. / Babar a loué une maison à Baribarbotton. Les enfants courent en avant, très excités. « Comme la mer est belle et la maison jolie! » dit Céleste contente d'être arrivée.

During the trip the three little elephants look out the window; Arthur signals to them. It is all very amusing. / Babar has rented a house in Baribarbotton. The children run on ahead in great excitement. "Oh, how beautiful the sea is! And the house is so pretty," says Celeste, happy to have arrived.

138

139

At the Beach

140

141

140. Study for p. 8.

141. Study for p. 8.

142. Study for p. 9.

143. Dummy for pp. 8–9.

A peine installée, toute la famille se dépêche d'aller sur la plage. Pom, Flore et Alexandre ne sont pas très rassurés. Babar les encourage: « Venez vous tremper avec moi, dit-il; nous allons jouer à nous arroser. Regardez comme Arthur est satisfait. » Ils se décident enfin, et bientôt ne voudront plus sortir de l'eau. / Zéphir emmène Flore en bateau. Il lui raconte une histoire qu'elle aime beaucoup: celle d'Eléonore la sirène et de la princesse Isabelle. « Ecoute » dit Flore quand l'histoire est finie, « je voudrais bien la voir, la petite sirène! » « Ce n'est pas possible, répond Zéphir, elle ne se dérange que si l'on a vraiment besoin d'elle. » En attendant leur tour pour la promenade en bateau, les deux garçons jouent avec leur père au jeu des petits paquets. Sur l'épaule! Sous le bras! Hop! Hop! Céleste est en train de préparer le goûter.

Hardly settled, the whole family hurries down to the beach. Pom, Flora, and Alexander are a bit worried. Babar reassures them: "Come take a dip with me," he says, "We'll romp and spray each other. See how Arthur loves it." Finally they agree to try it, and soon they don't want to get out of the water. / Zephir takes Flora out in a boat. He tells a story that delights her. It is about Eleanor, a mermaid, and the Princess Isabel. "Do you know what?" says Flora, at the end of the tale. "I'd love to see this little mermaid!" "Oh, that is impossible," replies Zephir, "she only appears when someone really needs her." While awaiting their turns for a ride in the boat, the two boys play with their father. They pretend they are little packages and he tosses them about, up on his shoulder, down under his arm. Hoopla! Hop! Celeste is preparing their afternoon snack.

142

143

Seaside Fun

144. Study for p. 10.

145. Study for p. 11.

146. Dummy for pp. 10–11.

Arthur est allé se promener tout seul, une idée en tête. Conduits par Zéphir, les trois petits vont pêcher la crevette. Pom et Alexandre poussent leur filet avec ardeur. / Flore préfère les crabes. « Venez voir les belles boucles d'oreilles! » crie-t-elle à ses frères. Zéphir a la peau moins dure et se fait pincer très fort. Mais où est donc Arthur?

Arthur went off by himself for a walk. He has an idea. Zephir now takes the three children off to fish for shrimp. Pom and Alexander eagerly sweep their nets around. / Flora prefers crabbing. She calls to her brothers, "Come and see the beautiful earrings!" Zephir, whose skin isn't as tough as hers, gets painfully nipped by the crabs. But where is Arthur?

A Magnificent Plane

147

148

147. Study for pp. 12–13.

148. Dummy for p. 12–13.

Il a découvert ce qu'il cherchait: le fameux camp d'aviation voisin. « Voilà qui est plus intéressant que la pêche! » pense-t-il en regardant de tous ses yeux. / Il n'a jamais vu tant d'avions à la fois: des avions rouges, des bleus, des noirs. Le plus beau de tous, c'est le vert. Arthur a bien envie de monter sur sa queue. . . .

He has found what he was looking for: the well-known airport nearby. "Here's something far more interesting than fishing!" he says to himself, as he takes it all in eagerly. / He has never seen so many planes all in one place: red planes, blue planes, black planes. But the most beautiful of all is the green plane. Arthur longs to climb up on its tail. . . .

149. Study for p. 14.

150. Study for p. 15.

151. Dummy for pp. 14–15.

Que s'est-il passé? Tous les éléphants courent, affolés, et regardent le grand avion vert qui vient de partir. Mais c'est Arthur qui est sur la queue! Il venait d'y grimper quand l'avion a commencé à rouler. Tremblant de peur, mais n'osant plus descendre, il s'est cramponné. Un éléphant l'a vu . . . Puis deux . . . Puis trois . . . Puis vingt. . . . / Ils crient tous à la fois: « Il va tomber! Il va tomber!—Non! Il a l'air de tenir!—Il doit s'accrocher avec sa trompe!—Il ne tiendra pas longtemps si personne ne vient à son secours!—C'est épouvantable!— Mais qui est-ce donc?—Le petit cousin de Babar!— On ne voit plus qu'un point rouge!—Il a disparu!—Est-il sauvé?—Allons tout de suite prévenir le roi Babar!—Il doit être sur la plage. »

What has happened? All the elephants run up, very frightened, as they look up at the big green plane that has just taken off. Arthur is on its tail! He had just climbed on when the plane started moving. Trembling with fear, but not daring to jump off, he hung on desperately. First one elephant saw him, then two . . . then three . . . then twenty . . . . / They all shout at the same time: "He'll fall off! He'll fall off!"—No! He seems to be holding on fast!—He must be holding on by his trunk!—He won't be able to stay on long unless someone comes to his rescue!—It's too terrible!— But who do you suppose it is?—It's Babar's little cousin!—All you can see is a little red speck in the distance!—He's disappeared altogether!—Is he safe?—Let's run and tell King Babar about it at once!—He must be down on the beach."

149

150

151

On Board

152

153

154

155

152. Study for p. 16.

153. Study for p. 16.

154. Study for p. 16.

155. Study for p. 16.

156. Study for p. 17.

157. Study for p. 17.

158. Dummy for pp. 16–17.
A la demande du pilote qui sent l'arrière alourdi, un voyageur se penche, aperçoit Arthur. Il croit rêver, et, retenant un cri: « Donne-moi ta trompe petit! lui dit-il; serre la mienne de toutes tes forces! Ho! Hisse! » Le vent siffle aux oreilles d'Arthur. . . . Il est sauvé! N'en pouvant plus[,] il entre péniblement par la fenêtre. / Remis de ses émotions, Arthur s'avance dans l'avion; les voyageurs le regardent. Le pilote est un rhinocéros, toujours de mauvaise humeur. « Qu'est-ce que c'est que cette histoire-là! grogne-t-il, tu seras puni pour ta bêtise! Je vais te donner un parachute. Tu trouveras le train en bas, chez les Arabes, pour retourner à Baribarbotton. »

At the request of the pilot, who feels that the plane is bottom-heavy, a passenger leans out. He sees Arthur. He thinks he must be dreaming. Not wanting to frighten Arthur, he whispers, "Give me your trunk, little one. Hold on to mine with all your might. Heave ho!" The wind whistles through Arthur's ears. . . . He is safe! Utterly exhausted, he painfully squeezes himself through the window. / After catching his breath, Arthur walks up the aisle while all the passengers stare at him. The pilot is a cranky rhinoceros, always in a bad humor. "What's going on here?" he growls. "You'll be punished for this silly nonsense! I'm going to give you a parachute. There's a train back to Baribarbotton down below, where the Arabs live."

156

157

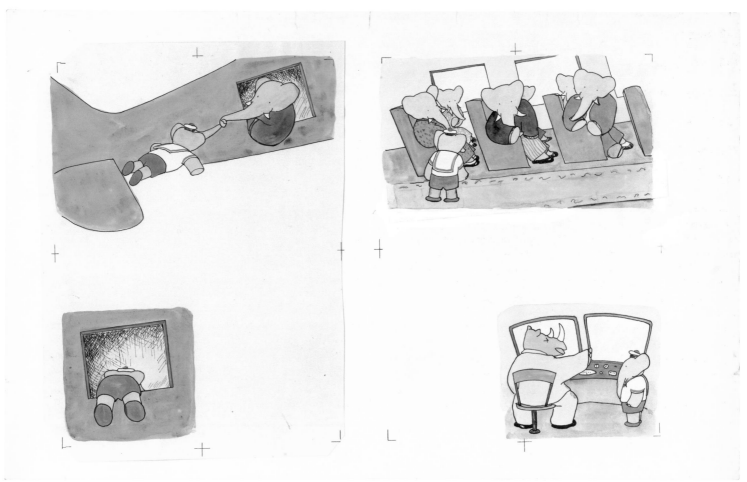

158

A Parachute Ride

159

160

161

159. Study for pp. 18–19.

160. Study for pp. 18–19.

161. Dummy for pp. 18–19.
Arthur a sauté. Il tombe comme une pierre. Mais brusquement le parachute s'ouvre! Que c'est drôle alors, une vraie balançoire! Le vent le pousse, en avant, en arrière. Il n'a jamais vu les nuages de si près. Et voici la terre qui se rapproche. . . .

Arthur has jumped. He drops like a stone. But suddenly his chute opens! My, how funny, just like a real swing! The wind blows him forward and backward. He has never seen the clouds up so close. And now the earth is coming up to meet him. . . .

162. Study for pp. 20–21.

163. Dummy for pp. 20–21.
Arthur ne voit pas d'Arabes, mais seulement une grande girafe, l'air étonné, et des bêtes bizarres qui lèvent la tête pour le regarder.

Arthur doesn't see any Arabs, but only a tall giraffe, who looks at him in astonishment, and some strange beasts who lift their heads to stare at him.

162

163

Arthur's New Friends

164

165

164. Study for p. 22.

165. Study for p. 23.

166. Study for pp. 22–23.

167. Dummy for pp. 22–23.
Arthur s'est débarrassé de son parachute. « C'est le pays des kangourous! » dit-il en reconnaissant ces drôles de bêtes. « Eh bien! On ne s'ennuie pas ici! » En effet, tous bavardent avec animation, courent, sautent, luttent, dansent, ou se poursuivent entre les arbres. Quelques-uns s'approchent d'Arthur et l'examinent avec curiosité.

Arthur has unstrapped his chute. "This must be the kangaroo country!" says he, as he recognizes these funny-looking animals. "Well, well, they all seem to be having a very good time here!" Sure enough, they're all chattering away gaily, running around, jumping, wrestling, and dancing as they chase one another among the trees. Some of them come up to Arthur and examine him curiously.

166

167

Clowning Around

168

169

168. Study for p. 24.

169. Study for p. 25.

170. Study for p. 24.

171. Dummy for pp. 24–25.

« Eh! gros oiseau, lui dit l'un d'eux, qui es-tu? D'où viens-tu? Raconte-nous ton voyage. » « Je ne suis pas un oiseau, répond Arthur, je ne sais pas voler, regardez. » Il agite les bras, saute, et retombe. « J'étais sur une machine qui vole, une énorme machine qui fait beaucoup de bruit. Vous m'avez vu sauter avec un parachute. » Il deviennent vite bons amis. A quatre pattes, Arthur joue avec les bébés, qui le trouvent très drôle. « Moi aussi j'ai une poche comme vos mamans! » dit-il en les mettant doucement dans son béret. Mais les mamans un peu inquiètes s'écrient: « ne les laissez pas tomber, surtout! Ils ne sont pas encore bien solides! »

"Hi, there, big bird, who are you?" says one. "Where do you come from? Tell us about your trip." "I'm not a bird," answers Arthur. "I can't fly. Look." He waves his arms, leaps up, and falls down. "I was on a flying machine, an enormous machine that makes a terrific noise. You saw me drift down by parachute." They quickly become good friends. Down on all fours, Arthur plays with the baby kangaroos, who think he's very funny. "Look I have a pouch, just like your mamas'!" he says, as he puts them gently in his beret. At this point, the mamas become a little anxious and cry out, "Oh, don't drop them! They're not very strong yet!"

170

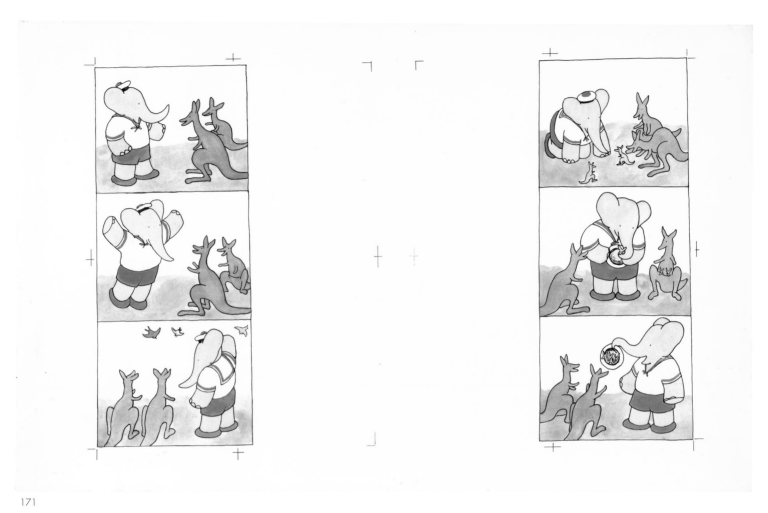

171

The Monkeys' Trick

172. Study for p. 26.

173. Study for p. 27.

174. Study for p. 27.

175. Dummy for pp. 26–27.
Mais il faut tout de même partir. Arthur songe à ce qui l'attend au retour: il sera certainement grondé pour être monté imprudemment sur l'avion. Assis autour de lui, les kangourous lui répètent: « Vous reviendrez, n'est-ce-pas, monsieur l'éléphant? » « Peut-être », répond Arthur qui regrette de quitter ses nouveaux amis. / Comme ce n'est pas un train pour éléphants, Arthur a été obligé de monter dans un wagon de marchandises. Il s'est endormi profondément. Dans la forêt, les petits singes ont l'habitude de sauter sur le toit des wagons. « Ho! Ho! » font-ils en découvrant Arthur, « nous allons lui jouer un bon tour! » Et ces polissons décrochent le wagon.

But all the same, Arthur realizes he must leave. He ponders what will happen when he gets back, for he will most surely be scolded for having so stupidly climbed up on the plane. Squatting around him, the kangaroos plead with him again and again, "You'll be sure to come back, won't you, Mr. Elephant?" "Perhaps I will," answers Arthur, who regrets having to leave his new friends. / As the train isn't meant for elephants, Arthur has to get into a freight car. He has fallen sound asleep. The little monkeys in the woods very often jump onto the roofs of the cars as they go by. "Ho! Ho!" they jabber as they discover Arthur. "We'll play a fine trick on him!" And the scamps uncouple the freight car.

174

175

Where Is Arthur?

176. Study for pp. 28–29.

177. Dummy for pp. 28–29.

« Ah! Malheureux que je suis! Que vais-je devenir? » s'écrie Arthur en se réveillant. Il entend des rires derrière les arbres, / Et comprend tout de suite ce qui s'est passé. Il décide d'attraper un des vilains singes pour lui donner une bonne correction.

"Oh, woe is me, what will become of me?" cries Arthur, as he wakes up. He hears laughter from behind the trees / and realizes at once what has happened. He decides to catch one of these villainous monkeys and punish him severely.

178. Study for p. 30.

179. Dummy for pp. 30–31.

Pendant ce temps-là, Babar et Céleste s'inquiètent: voilà deux jours qu'Arthur a disparu. De leur côté, Pom, Flore, Alexandre et Zéphir se demandent ce qu'il est devenu. / Babar appelle le pilote de l'avion vert et lui dit: « A quel endroit Arthur a-t-il sauté en parachute? Par ta faute, il est peut-être arrivé malheur à ce petit! » « Nous passions au-dessus d'el Talahil, » répond le rhinocéros très ennuyé. « Eh bien! dit Babar, je vais aller le chercher. » Il prend son casque colonial à cause des coups de soleil, un gros manteau pour les nuits froides, et s'apprête à traverser le désert en autochenille.

Meanwhile Babar and Celeste have become very worried. It has been two whole days since Arthur disappeared. As for Pom, Flora, Alexander, and Zephir, they wonder what could have happened to their cousin. / Babar sends for the pilot of the green airplane and says, "Tell me, exactly where did Arthur jump by parachute? Something serious may have happened to this young man and, if so, it's your fault!" "We were flying over El Talahil," answers the rhinoceros, very much embarrassed. "Very well!" says Babar, "I'm going out to search for him." He takes his tropical helmet to protect him from sunburn, a heavy overcoat for cold nights, and prepares to cross the desert by caterpillar tractor.

178

179

By the Riverbank

180

181

180. Study for p. 32.

181. Study for p. 32.

182. Study for p. 33.

183. Study for p. 33.

184. Dummy for p. 32.
Arthur n'a pas pu attraper les singes. Ils se sont moqués de lui en sautant d'arbre en arbre. Ayant atteint le bord d'un fleuve, il s'assied, penaud, fourbu, et réfléchit. Voilà qu'il aperçoit deux dromadaires en train de boire un peu plus loin. Il va les trouver et leur dit: « Bonjour messieurs. Je m'appelle Arthur; je suis le petit cousin de Babar le roi des éléphants. »

Arthur wasn't able to catch the monkeys. They laughed at him as they swung from tree to tree. Having reached the banks of a river, he sits down crestfallen and dead tired, to think things over. At a little distance, he notices two dromedaries, drinking water. He goes over to them and says, "Good day, sirs. My name is Arthur. I'm the little cousin of Babar, King of the Elephants."

185. Dummy for p. 33.
« Vous serait-il possible de me ramener au bord de la mer, à Baribarbotton, car je me suis perdu? »

"Would it be possible for you to take me back to the seashore at Baribarbotton? I am lost."

182

183

184

185

A Bridge of Hippopotami

186

187

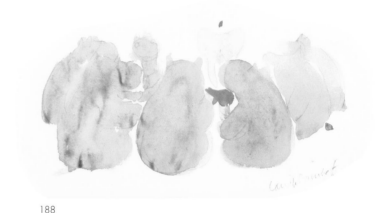

188

186. Study for p. 34.

187. Study for pp. 34–35.

188. Study for p. 35.

189. Study for pp. 36, 38, or cover.

190. Dummy for pp. 34–35.

Les dromadaires lui ont répondu qu'ils étaient justement en train de faire leur provision d'eau pour un long voyage et qu'un petit détour ne les ennuierait pas. Mais il faut traverser le fleuve où nagent des crocodiles féroces, et les dromadaires ont peur de se faire couper les jambes. / Heureusement, un brave hippopotame voit leur embarras. « Eh! Jeune éléphant, dit-il à Arthur, Je peux t'aider à traverser le fleuve, ce n'est pas difficile. Avec tous mes amis, qu'il suffit d'appeler, nous allons rapidement faire un pont. Permettez-moi de vous présenter d'abord mon frère Boudu. »

The dromedaries reply that they were just taking their supply of water for a long journey. A short detour wouldn't bother them. But they would have to cross the river, and there were ferocious crocodiles. The dromedaries were afraid they might have their legs bitten off. / Luckily a brave hippopotamus sees their plight and says to Arthur, "See here, Little Elephant, I can help you get across the river. That's easy. What with all my friends, I only have to call them, and we'll quickly make a bridge. First allow me to introduce you to my brother, Boudu."

191. Dummy for pp. 36–37.

Et voici le pont d'hippopotames. / Les crocodiles sont furieux.

And here is the bridge of hippos. / The crocodiles are furious.

189

Prendre comme jaune l'éventail le ni de Brunhoff en points

On the Road

192

193

192. Study for p. 38.

193. Study for p. 38.

194. Study for p. 39.

195. Dummy for pp. 38–39.

Le fleuve est traversé. Les trois voyageurs s'enfoncent dans le désert, et marchent jusqu'au soir. La nuit tombée, ils se reposent. / Il fait vraiment très chaud. Arthur demande un petit arrêt aux dromadaires pour s'asseoir dans leur ombre. Ils commencent à être fatigués.

The river is crossed. The three travelers start across the desert. They travel till dark. When night falls they lie down to rest. / It is really very hot. Arthur begs the dromedaries for a brief halt, so as to sit down in their shadow. They are getting tired.

194

195

At Last, a Town

196

197

196. Study for p. 40.

197. Study for p. 41.

198. Study for pp. 40–41.

199. Dummy for pp. 40–41.
Ils arrivent enfin dans un village arabe. Le voyage s'est bien passé: quand un dromadaire avait mal à la bosse, Arthur montait sur l'autre. Maintenant il est descendu pour se dégourdir les jambes. Mais la soif lui dessèche toute la trompe. Il faut absolument trouver un puits. / Un vieux monsieur à barbe lui a indiqué l'endroit où il pourrait calmer sa soif. Arthur a déjà bu deux seaux d'eau plein jusqu'au bord. Tout à coup il s'étrangle presque: il vient d'apercevoir Babar au bout de la rue, qui court vers lui le plus vite possible, en faisant de grands gestes.

At last they arrive at an Arab village. The trip has gone very well, for when one of the dromedaries had a sore back, Arthur rode on the other. Now he gets off to stretch his own legs. He is very thirsty. The entire length of his trunk is dry. They must find a well. / A bearded old gentleman has pointed out to him where he can quench his thirst. Arthur has already had two pails of water, full to the brim. All of a sudden he nearly chokes. He has caught sight of Babar at the end of the street, running toward him as fast as he can, waving wildly.

198

199

A Joyful Reunion

200. Study for p. 42.

201. Study for p. 43.

202. Dummy for pp. 42–43.

Arthur se jette dans les bras de Babar. Ils s'embrassent de toutes leurs forces. Quelle joie de se retrouver enfin! Mais il faut tout de même gronder. Arthur baisse la tête. Sûrement il n'aura plus jamais d'aussi mauvaises idées. Après avoir beaucoup remercié les dromadaires de leur gentillesse, Babar emmène Arthur avec lui. / « Partons, dit-il, Céleste est très inquiète; retournons vite à Baribarbotton. Mon autochenille est au coin de la rue. Mais viens d'abord manger quelquechose chez mon ami Moustapha. Il est très gentil. » Tout en marchant Babar continue: « Voyons mon petit Arthur, je te croyais devenu un grand garçon! Si Pom ou Alexandre faisaient une bêtise pareille, je comprendrais, mais toi, allons! »

Arthur throws himself into Babar's arms. They embrace each other heartily. What joy to be reunited at last! Even so, the time has come for a scolding. Arthur hangs his head. Surely he'd never have such foolish ideas again. After thanking the dromedaries warmly for their kindness, Babar takes young Arthur back home with him. / "Let's go," says he. "Celeste is very worried. Let's get back to Baribarbotton as fast as possible. My tractor is at the street corner. But now come and have something to eat at my old friend Moustapha's. He is very nice." As they walk along, Babar continues to scold. "Really, my little Arthur, I thought you were a big boy! If Pom or Alexander did something as stupid as this, I'd understand, but you, really!"

202

Moustapha's Feast

203

203. Study for pp. 44–45.

204. Dummy for pp. 44–45.

Moustapha et ses deux fils leur ont offert un repas
savoureux. Pour le dessert, il y a des oranges, /
des bananes et de délicieux gâteaux au miel,
appelés « cornes de gazelle ». Rassasié, Arthur
devient bavard.

Moustapha and his two sons served a tasty meal.
For dessert there are oranges / and bananas and
delicious honey cakes called "gazelles' horns."
Having eaten his fill, Arthur becomes talkative.

204

Return to Baribarbotton

205

206

205. Study for p. 46.

206. Study for p. 47.

207. Dummy for pp. 46–47.
Leurs hôtes les ont reconduits poliment jusqu'à la sortie du village où Babar avait laissé la voiture. Il met le moteur en marche. Assis confortablement sur la banquette, Arthur se sent bien. « Décidément, se dit-il, j'aime mieux les voyages en auto. » / Ils arrivent au bord de la mer. Babar a klaxonné et toute la famille, sortant de la maison, se précipite à leur rencontre. Pom, le premier, monte sur l'auto. « Te voilà tout de même, vieux camarade! » dit Zéphir.

Their hosts politely conduct them to the outskirts of the village, where Babar had parked the tractor. He steps on the starter. Seated comfortably on the back seat, Arthur feels fine. "There's no doubt about it," he says to himself, "I prefer traveling by car." / They arrive at the seashore. Babar has tooted his horn, and the whole family rushes out to greet them. Pom reaches the car first and climbs on. "Well, here you are, after all, old fellow!" says Zephir.

208

208. Study for p. 48.

209. Dummy for p. 48.
Ce soir-là Arthur est si fatigué qu'il s'endort tout habillé sur son lit. Doucement, pour ne pas le réveiller, Céleste vient lui mettre un pyjama. Elle est bien heureuse de le voir à nouveau parmi eux.

That night, Arthur is so tired that he falls asleep on his bed with all his clothes on. Softly, so as not to wake him, Celeste comes in to put him in his pajamas. She is very happy to have him back again.

48

Checklist of Manuscripts, Drawings, and Illustrations

All drawings and manuscripts for Jean de Brunhoff's *Histoire de Babar, le petit éléphant* (MA 6304) reproduced in this catalogue are from the collection of The Morgan Library & Museum; gift of Laurent, Mathieu, and Thierry de Brunhoff and purchased with the assistance of The Florence Gould Foundation and the Acquisitions Fund, Fellows Endowment Fund, Gordon N. Ray Fund, and Heineman Fund, 2004. All drawings for Laurent de Brunhoff's *Babar et ce coquin d'Arthur* (MA 6305) are from the collection of The Morgan Library & Museum; gift of Laurent de Brunhoff, 2004. Pages from the first French edition of *Histoire de Babar, le petit éléphant* (Paris: Editions du Jardin des modes, 1931) are reproduced from the Morgan's copy, PML 83295, purchased on the Elisabeth Ball Fund, 1978.

Cover

Jean de Brunhoff, *Histoire de Babar, le petit éléphant.* Variant drawing and text for pp. 6–7, detail. For full image, see No. 16.
MA 6304.9.2.

Half-title page

Laurent de Brunhoff, *Babar et ce coquin d'Arthur.* Study for p. 43, detail. For full image, see No. 201.
MA 6305.1.37.

Title page

Jean de Brunhoff, *Histoire de Babar, le petit éléphant.* Dummy for p. 37, detail. For full image, see No. 100.
MA 6304.10.23 (recto).

Copyright page

Jean de Brunhoff, *Histoire de Babar, le petit éléphant.* Dummy for p. 8, detail. For full image, see No. 17.
MA 6304.10.06 (verso).

Table of contents

Jean de Brunhoff, *Histoire de Babar, le petit éléphant.* Dummy for p. 29, detail. For full image, see No. 74.
MA 6304.10.19 (recto).

Director's Foreword, pp. vi–ix

Detail on p. vi: Laurent de Brunhoff, *Babar et ce coquin d'Arthur.* Dummy for pp. 20–21. For full image, see No. 163.

Fig. 1. Checklist of an exhibition of the work of Jean de Brunhoff. Durlacher Brothers, New York, 24 March–30 April 1938.
The Morgan Library & Museum, acquired with PML 83298. Purchased on the Elisabeth Ball Fund, 1978.

Fig. 2. Checklist of an exhibition of the work of Balthus. Pierre Matisse Gallery, New York, 21 March–16 April 1938.
The Morgan Library & Museum, Pierre Matisse Gallery Archives, MA 5020. Gift of the Pierre Matisse Foundation, 1997.

Freeing the Elephants, pp. 1–15

Details on p. 1 (and facing page): Jean de Brunhoff, *Histoire de Babar, le petit éléphant.* Dummy for p. 9. For full image, see No 18.
MA 6304.10.06 (verso).

Fig. 1. Henri Rousseau, *The Sleeping Gypsy*, 1897.
Oil on canvas.
The Museum of Modern Art.

Fig. 2. Henri Matisse, *The Painter's Family*, Issy-les-Moulineaux, 1911. Oil on canvas.
The State Hermitage Museum. © 2008 Succession H. Matisse / Artists Rights Society (ARS), New York.

Fig. 3. Henri Matisse, *The Piano Lesson*, Issy-les-Moulineaux, late summer 1916. Oil on canvas.
The Museum of Modern Art. © 2008 Succession H. Matisse / Artists Rights Society (ARS), New York.

Fig. 4. Henri Matisse, *The Moroccans*, Issy-les-Moulineaux, late 1915 and fall 1916. Oil on canvas.
The Museum of Modern Art. © 2008 Succession H. Matisse / Artists Rights Society (ARS), New York.

Fig. 5. Jean de Brunhoff, *Le roi Babar*, Paris: Editions du Jardin des modes, 1933; p. 25.

The Morgan Library & Museum, PML 83296. Purchased on the Elisabeth Ball Fund, 1978.

Fig. 6. Jean de Brunhoff, *Le roi Babar*, Paris: Editions du Jardin des modes, 1933; pp. 44–45.
The Morgan Library & Museum, PML 83296. Purchased on the Elisabeth Ball Fund, 1978.

Babar in Progress, pp. 16–45

Detail on p. 16: Laurent de Brunhoff, *Babar et ce coquin d'Arthur*. Dummy for pp. 14–15. For full image, see No. 151.
MA 6304.4.08.

Fig. 1. Family photograph of Cécile, Jean, Laurent, and Mathieu de Brunhoff, ca. 1931.
Van Hamel Family Archives.

Fig. 2. Jean de Brunhoff, pen-and-ink study for the cover of *Babar et le Père Noël*, 1936. Color by Laurent de Brunhoff, ca. 1940.
Courtesy of Laurent, Mathieu, and Thierry de Brunhoff.

Fig. 3. Rudyard Kipling, "The Elephant's Child," in *Just So Stories for Little Children*. London: Macmillan & Co., 1902, p. 73.
The Morgan Library & Museum, PML 129913. Gift of S. Parker Gilbert, 2007.

Fig. 4. Reginald Rigby, *The Absurd Story of James*. London: Knight Brothers, 1905, p. [2].
Cotsen Children's Library. Department of Rare Books and Special Collections, Princeton University Library, Cotsen 2856.

Fig. 5. H. G. Wells, *The Adventures of Tommy*. London: The Amalgamated Press, 1928, p. [35].
Cotsen Children's Library. Department of Rare Books and Special Collections, Princeton University Library, Cotsen 18135.

Figs. 6–7. Onkel Franz (pseudonym of Erich Mühsam and H. H. Ewers), illustrated by Paul Haase, *Billy's Erdengang: Eine Elephantengeschichte für artige Kinder*. Berlin: Globus Verlag, [1904], cover and unnumbered page.
Cotsen Children's Library. Department of Rare Books and Special Collections, Princeton University Library, Cotsen 40081.

Fig. 8. Jean de Brunhoff, *Histoire de Babar, le petit éléphant*. Watercolor illustration and autograph text for p. 37, 1930 or 1931.
The Morgan Library & Museum, MA 6304.10.23 (recto).

Fig. 9. *Zōtarō*. Tokyo: Dai Nihon Yūbenkai Kōdansha, 1929, unpaginated.
Cotsen Children's Library. Department of Rare Books and Special Collections, Princeton University Library, Cotsen 62290.

Fig. 10. A. A. Milne, decorations by Ernest H. Shepard, *Winnie-the-Pooh*. London: Methuen & Co., 1926, p. 62.
The Morgan Library & Museum, PML 83198. Purchased as the gift of Avery Fisher, 1989.

Fig. 11. Louise-Maurice Boutet de Monvel, *Jeanne d'Arc*. Paris: Plon-Nourriet & Cie., 1896, p. 6.
The Morgan Library & Museum, PML 140762. Bequest of Gordon N. Ray, 1987.

Figs. 12–13. André Hellé, *Drôles de bêtes*. Paris. A. Tolmer et Cie., [1910s], cover and unnumbered page.
Cotsen Children's Library. Department of Rare Books and Special Collections, Princeton University Library, Cotsen 6824.

Fig. 14. Edy Legrand, *Macao & Cosmage, ou l'experience du bonheur*. Paris: Editions de la Nouvelle Revue Française, [1919], unnumbered page.
The Morgan Library & Museum, PML 141621. Bequest of Gordon N. Ray, 1987.

Fig. 15. *L'Effervescence et l'amour maternel, ou, Histoire de Prince Ardelin*. Illustrated manuscript by an unidentified author, 1779, illustration no. 11 (mounted between pp. 57 and 58).
The Morgan Library & Museum, MA 4090. Purchased on the Fellows Fund, 1985.

Fig. 16. *La Sainte Bible (Ancien Testament)*, illustrated by J. James Tissot. Paris: M. de Brun[h]off & Cie., 1904, copy 1, title page of vol. 1.
The Morgan Library & Museum, PML 195000.

Fig. 17. Cover of 1911 program for the ballet *Narcisse* at the Théatre du Châtelet, Paris, with illustration by Léon Bakst, in *Collection des plus beaux numéros de Comœdia illustré et des programmes consacrés aux Ballets & Galas Russes depuis le début à Paris*, 1909–1921. Paris: M. de Brun[h]off, [1922?].
The Morgan Library & Museum, PMC 428. The Mary Flagler Cary Collection.

Fig. 18. *Le jardin des modes*. Paris: Groupe des publications Condé Nast, 15 August 1930, cover. Special Collections, Gladys Marcus Library, Fashion Institute of Technology-SUNY.

Fig. 19. Jean de Brunhoff, *Histoire de Babar, le petit éléphant*. Paris: Editions du Jardin des modes, 1931, p. 41. The Morgan Library & Museum, PML 83295. Purchased on the Elisabeth Ball Fund, 1978.

Fig. 20. Jean de Brunhoff, back endpapers from the maquette for *Histoire de Babar, le petit éléphant*, 1930 or 1931. The Morgan Library & Museum, MA 6304.1, pp. 38–39.

Fig. 21. Jean de Brunhoff, Color notes for *Histoire de Babar, le petit éléphant*, 1930 or 1931. The Morgan Library & Museum, MA 6304.2.6.

Fig. 22. Gustave Gabet and George Gillard, illustrated by Ferdinand Raffin, *Vocabulaire et méthode d'orthographie*. Paris: Librairie Hachette, 1935, p. 4. Cotsen Children's Library. Department of Rare Books and Special Collections, Princeton University Library, Cotsen 92905.

Fig. 23. Jean de Brunhoff, *Histoire de Babar, le petit éléphant*. Watercolor illustration and autograph text for p. 6, 1930 or 1931. The Morgan Library & Museum, MA 6304.10.05 (verso).

Fig. 24. Robert Kretschmer, "Auf der Elephantenjagd in Abyssinien," in *Die Gartenlaube*. Leipzig: Ernst Keil, 1862, p. 501.

Figs. 25–26. Jean de Brunhoff, *Histoire de Babar, le petit éléphant*. Illustrations (one printed, one watercolor) and autograph text for pp. 46–47, 1930 or 1931. The Morgan Library & Museum, MA 6304.10.27 (verso) and MA 6304.10.28 (recto).

Figs. 27–28. Antoine de Saint-Exupéry, *Le petit prince*. New York: Reynal & Hitchcock, 1943, pp. 90 and 92. The Morgan Library & Museum, PML 84864. Purchased on the Elisabeth Ball Fund, 1986.

Figs. 29–32. Jean de Brunhoff, *Histoire de Babar, le petit éléphant*. Pencil drafts for chapter divisions, 1930 or 1931. The Morgan Library & Museum, MA 6304.7.1–4.

Fig. 33. Laurent de Brunhoff, *Babar et ce coquin d'Arthur*. Various drafts for detail on pp. 4–5, 1946, and page from the first edition (Paris: Hachette, 1946). The Morgan Library & Museum, MA 6305.1.02 (verso), MA 6305.1.03, MA 6305.1.04, MA 6305.1.05 (verso), MA 6305.1.05, MA 6305.2.05, and MA 6305.4.03; PML 86479, purchased on the Elisabeth Ball Fund, 2005.

Figs. 34–35. Laurent de Brunhoff, *Babar et ce coquin d'Arthur*. Watercolor draft and final illustration for detail on pp. 28–29, 1946. The Morgan Library & Museum, MA 6305.1.27 (verso) and MA 6305.4.15.

Fig. 36. Laurent de Brunhoff, *Babar et ce coquin d'Arthur*. Watercolor illustration for pp. 14–15, 1946. The Morgan Library & Museum, MA 6305.4.08.

Fig. 37. Edy Legrand, *Macao & Cosmage, ou l'experience du bonheur*. Paris: Editions de la Nouvelle Revue Française, [1919], unnumbered page. The Morgan Library & Museum, PML 141621. Bequest of Gordon N. Ray, 1987.

Fig. 38. Antoine de Saint-Exupéry, Watercolor illustration for *Le petit prince*, ca. 1943, not included in printed edition. The Morgan Library & Museum, MA 2592.143. Purchased on the Elisabeth Ball Fund, 1968.

Figs. 39–40. André Boursier-Mougenot, *Doudou s'envole*. Paris: Tours Maison Mame, 1934, cover and unnumbered page. Cotsen Children's Library. Department of Rare Books and Special Collections, Princeton University Library, Cotsen 10626.

Fig. 41. Beatrix Potter, *The Tale of Peter Rabbit*. London: Frederick Warne & Co., 1901; frontispiece. (Photograph made from the fourth printing of the first edition, published after 1903.) The Morgan Library & Museum, JPW 1103. Gift of Julia P. Wightman, 1991.

Fig. 42. Laurent de Brunhoff, *Babar et ce coquin d'Arthur*. Watercolor illustration for p. 48, 1946. The Morgan Library & Museum, MA 6305.4.26.

CATALOGUE
Jean de Brunhoff's *Histoire de Babar, le petit éléphant,* pp. 46–101

Detail on p. 47: Jean de Brunhoff. *Histoire de Babar, le petit éléphant.* Study for the character Babar. MA 6304.8.4.

Jean de Brunhoff's surviving sketches and manuscripts have been arranged in the following groups:

MA 6304.1
Maquette (36 numbered pages plus additional front and back matter). Graphite with occasional crayon and watercolor. Approx. 8¼ × 6¼ inches (20.5 × 15.8 cm); dimensions of individual pages vary slightly.
    See Fig. 20 on p. 28 and Nos. 3, 5–7, 13, 19, 25, 29, 32, 37, 41, 44, 50, 53, 56–57, 62–63, 69, 75, 81, 86, 90, 98, 101, 105, 110, 124.

MA 6304.2
Manuscript notes on color (11 pp.). 8 × 6 inches (20.5 × 15.5 cm).
    See Fig. 21 on p. 29. Other pages not pictured.

MA 6304.3
Studies for text and illustrations (15 pp. on 14 sheets). Graphite, with occasional pen and watercolor trials. Written on paper torn from a notebook with dot-perforated left edge. 13 × 10½ inches (32.8 × 26.7 cm), with slight variations in width due to uneven tearing.
    See Nos. 14, 20, 26, 30, 33, 38, 42, 64, 70, 76–77, 85, 87, 102, 113.

MA 6304.4
Studies for text and illustrations (12 pp. on 11 sheets). Graphite. Written on newsprint paper torn from a notebook with perforated left edge. 13 × 9¾ inches (32.8 × 24.7 cm), with variations in width due to uneven tearing.
    See Nos. 34, 45, 51, 54, 58, 65, 67, 71, 83, 88, 99, 112.

MA 6304.5
Studies for text and illustrations (25 pp. on 20 sheets). Graphite, with occasional black and gray wash and pen and brush trials. Written on paper torn from a notebook with dot-perforated left edge and radius corners. 13½ × 10½ inches (34.5 × 26.9 cm).
    See Nos. 10, 21–22, 46, 49, 59–60, 66, 72–73, 78, 82, 91–93, 96–97, 106, 114–15, 117–18, 122. Not pictured: MA 6304.5.12 (verso; study for illustration on pp. 28–29), MA 6304.5.18 (study for illustration on pp. 44–45).

MA 6304.6
Studies for text and illustrations (4 pp.). Graphite. 8¼ × 6¼ inches (20.5 × 15.5 cm).
    Not pictured: MA 6304.6.1–2 (studies for illustrations on pp. 6–7), MA 6304.6.3–4 (studies for illustrations on pp. 20–21).

MA 6304.7
Studies for chapter headings (4 pp.). Graphite. 6¾ × 5¼ inches (17 × 13.5 cm).
See Figs. 29–32 on p. 34.

MA 6304.8
Studies for illustrations (4 pp.). Watercolor. Drawn on paper torn from a notebook with dot-perforated left edge and radius corners. 14⅜ × 10½ inches (36.5 × 26.7 cm). See No. 15 and detail on p. 47. Not pictured: MA 6304.8.1–2 (studies for p. 6, nearly identical to No. 15).

MA 6304.9
Variant studies for cover and illustrations (4 pp.). Watercolor, ink, and graphite. 14½ × 10⅜ inches (37 × 26.5 cm). See Nos. 2, 16, 121, 125.

MA 6304.10
Printer's dummy, comprising finished drawings and text, cut out, mounted to backings, and used for printing (50 pp. on 28 sheets). Watercolor and ink. 14⅛ × 10⅜ inches (36 × 26.5 cm).
    See Nos. 1, 4, 8, 11–12, 17–18, 23, 27–28, 31–32, 35, 40, 43, 47, 52, 61, 74, 79–80, 84, 89, 95, 100, 103–4, 107, 111, 119–20, 123. Items not pictured: MA 6304.10.03 (recto and verso; dummies for title and copyright pages), MA 6304.10.04 (verso) and MA 6304.10.05 (recto; dummies, lacking illustrations, for pp. 4–5), MA 6304.10.08 (recto; dummy, lacking illustration, for p. 11), MA 6304.10.11 (verso; dummy, lacking upper illustration, for p. 18), MA 6304.10.16 (recto; dummy, lacking illustration, for p. 23), MA 6304.10.17 (recto; dummy, lacking illustration, for p. 25), MA 6304.10.18 (recto; dummy, lacking illustration, for p. 27), MA 6304.10.21 (verso; dummy, lacking illustration, for p. 34), MA 6304.10.25 (recto; dummy, lacking illustration, for p. 41), MA 6304.10.26 (verso) and MA 6304.10.27 (recto; dummies, lacking illustrations, for pp. 44–45).

No. 1. MA 6304.10.01. Dummy for cover.
No. 2. MA 6304.9.1. Variant illustration for cover.
No. 3. MA 6304.01. Maquette, front cover.
No. 4. MA 6304.10.02. Dummy for endpapers.
No. 5. MA 6304.01. Maquette, front endpaper.

No. 6. MA 6304.01. Maquette, back cover.

No. 7. MA 6304.01. Maquette, title page.

No. 8. MA 6304.10.04 (recto). Dummy for p. 3.

No. 9. PML 83295. First edition, pp. 4–5.

No. 10. MA 6304.5.01 (recto). Study for pp. 4–5.

No. 11. MA 6304.10.05 (verso). Dummy for p. 6.

No. 12. MA 6304.10.06 (recto). Dummy for p. 7.

No. 13. MA 6304.01. Maquette, p. 1 (corresponding to pp. 6–7 of published book).

No. 14. MA 6304.3.01. Study for pp. 6–7.

No. 15. MA 6304.8.3. Study for p. 6.

No. 16. MA 6304.9.2. Variant drawing and text for pp. 6–7.

No. 17. MA 6304.10.06 (verso). Dummy for p. 8.

No. 18. MA 6304.10.07 (recto). Dummy for p. 9.

No. 19. MA 6304.01. Maquette, pp. 2–3 (corresponding to pp. 8–9 of published book).

No. 20. MA 6304.3.02. Study for pp. 8–9.

No. 21. MA 6304.5.02. Study for pp. 8–9.

No. 22. MA 6304.5.03. Study for pp. 8–9.

No. 23. MA 6304.10.07 (verso). Dummy for p. 10.

No. 24. PML 83295. First edition, p. 11.

No. 25. MA 6304.01. Maquette, pp. 4–5 (corresponding to pp. 10–11 of published book).

No. 26. MA 6304.3.03. Study for pp. 10–11.

No. 27. MA 6304.10.08 (verso). Dummy for p. 12.

No. 28. MA 6304.10.09 (recto). Dummy for p. 13.

No. 29. MA 6304.01. Maquette, pp. 6–7 (corresponding to pp. 12–13 of published book).

No. 30. MA 6304.3.04. Study for pp. 12–13.

No. 31. MA 6304.10.09 (verso) and MA 6304.10.10 (recto). Dummy for pp. 14–15.

No. 32. MA 6304.01. Maquette, pp. 8–9 (corresponding to pp. 14–15 of published book).

No. 33. MA 6304.3.05. Study for pp. 14–15.

No. 34. MA 6304.4.01. Study for pp. 14–15.

No. 35. MA 6304.10.10 (verso). Dummy for p. 16.

No. 36. MA 6304.10.11 (recto). Dummy for p. 17.

No. 37. MA 6304.01. Maquette, pp. 10–11 (corresponding to pp. 16–17 of published book).

No. 38. MA 6304.3.06. Study for p. 16.

No. 39. PML 83295. First edition, p. 18.

No. 40. MA 6304.10.12. Dummy for p. 19.

No. 41. MA 6304.01. Maquette, pp. 12–13 (corresponding to pp. 18–19 of published book).

No. 42. MA 6304.3.07. Study for p. 18.

No. 43. MA 6304.10.13–14. Dummy for pp. 20–21.

No. 44. MA 6304.01. Maquette, p. 15 (corresponding to pp. 20–21 of published book).

No. 45. MA 6304.4.02. Study for pp. 20–21.

No. 46. MA 6304.5.04. Study for pp. 20–21.

No. 47. MA 6304.10.15. Dummy for p. 22.

No. 48. MA 6304.5.05 (recto). Study for p. 22.

No. 49. PML 83295. First edition, p. 23.

No. 50. MA 6304.01. Maquette, p. 14 (corresponding to p. 23 of published book).

No. 51. MA 6304.4.03. Study for p. 23.

No. 52. MA 6304.10.16 (verso). Dummy for p. 24.

No. 53. MA 6304.01. Maquette, p. 16 (corresponding to p. 24 of published book).

No. 54. MA 6304.4.04. Study for p. 24.

No. 55. PML 83295. First edition, p. 25.

No. 56. MA 6304.01. Maquette, p. 17 (not included in published book but related to p. 25).

No. 57. MA 6304.01. Maquette, p. 18 (corresponding to p. 25 of published book).

No. 58. MA 6304.4.05. Study for p. 25.

No. 59. MA 6304.5.06. Study for p. 25.

No. 60. MA 6304.5.01 (verso). Draft of text for p. 25.

No. 61. MA 6304.10.17 (verso). Dummy for p. 26.

No. 62. MA 6304.01. Maquette, p. 19 (corresponding to upper portion of p. 26 of published book).

No. 63. MA 6304.01. Maquette, p. 20 (corresponding to p. 26 of published book).

No. 64. MA 6304.3.08. Study for p. 26.

No. 65. MA 6304.4.06. Study for p. 26.

No. 66. MA 6304.5.07. Study for p. 26.

No. 67. MA 6304.4.07. Study for p. 26.

No. 68. PML 83295. First edition, p. 27.

No. 69. MA 6304.01. Maquette, p. 21 (corresponding to p. 27 of published book).

No. 70. MA 6304.3.09. Study for p. 27.

No. 71. MA 6304.4.08. Study for p. 27.

No. 72. MA 6304.5.08 (recto). Study for p. 27.

No. 73. MA 6304.5.08 (verso). Study for p. 27.

No. 74. MA 6304.10.18 (verso) and MA 6304.10.19 (recto). Dummy for pp. 28–29.

No. 75. MA 6304.01. Maquette, pp. 22–23 (corresponding to pp. 28–29 of published book).

No. 76. MA 6304.3.10 (recto). Study for p. 29.

No. 77. MA 6304.3.10 (verso). Study for p. 29.

No. 78. MA 6304.5.09. Study for pp. 28–29.

No. 79. MA 6304.10.19 (verso). Dummy for p. 30.

No. 80. MA 6304.10.20 (recto). Dummy for p. 31.

No. 81. MA 6304.01. Maquette, pp. 24–25 (corresponding to p. 30 of published book).

No. 82. MA 6304.5.10 (recto). Study for pp. 30–31.

No. 83. MA 6304.4.09 (verso). Draft of text for pp. 20–21 and 30.

No. 84. MA 6304.10.20 (verso). Dummy for p. 32.

No. 85. MA 6304.3.11. Study for p. 32.

No. 86. MA 6304.01. Maquette, pp. 26–27 (corresponding to pp. 32–33 of published book).

No. 87. MA 6304.3.12. Study for pp. 32–33.

No. 88. MA 6304.4.09 (recto). Study for p. 33.

No. 89. MA 6304.10.21 (recto). Dummy for p. 33.

No. 90. MA 6304.01. Maquette, p. 28 (corresponding to p. 33 of published book).

No. 91. MA 6304.5.10 (verso). Study for p. 33.

No. 92. MA 6304.5.12 (recto). Study for pp. 32–33.

No. 93. MA 6304.5.11. Study for pp. 32–33.

No. 94. PML 83295. First edition, p. 34.

No. 95. MA 6304.10.22 (recto). Dummy for p. 35.

No. 96. MA 6304.5.13. Study for p. 34.

No. 97. MA 6304.5.14. Study for p. 34.

No. 98. MA 6304.01. Maquette, p. 29 (corresponding to p. 35 of published book).

No. 99. MA 6304.4.10. Study for p. 35.

No. 100. MA 6304.10.22 (verso) and MA 6304.10.23 (recto). Dummy for pp. 36–37.

No. 101. MA 6304.01. Maquette, pp. 30–31 (corresponding to pp. 36–37 of published book).

No. 102. MA 6304.3.13. Study for p. 37.

No. 103. MA 6304.10.23 (verso). Dummy for p. 38.

No. 104. MA 6304.10.24 (recto). Dummy for p. 39.

No. 105. MA 6304.01. Maquette, pp. 32–33 (corresponding to pp. 38–39 of published book).

No. 106. MA 6304.5.15. Study for p. 39.

No. 107. MA 6304.10.24 (verso). Dummy for p. 40.

No. 108. PML 83295. First edition, p. 41.

No. 109. MA 6304.10.25 (verso). Dummy for p. 42.

No. 110. MA 6304.01. Maquette, pp. 34–35 (corresponding to p. 42 and 44–45 of published book).

No. 111. MA 6304.10.26 (recto). Dummy for p. 43.

No. 112. MA 6304.4.11. Study for p. 43.

No. 113. MA 6304.3.14. Study for p. 43.

No. 114. MA 6304.5.16. Study for p. 43.

No. 115. MA 6304.5.17. Study for p. 43.

No. 116. PML 83295. First edition, pp. 44–45.

No. 117. MA 6304.5.19. Study for pp. 44–45.

No. 118. MA 6304.5.05 (verso). Draft of text for pp. 44–45.

No. 119. MA 6304.10.27 (verso). Dummy for p. 46. The illustration on this page is printed rather than drawn in ink, unlike all the other dummy illustrations.

No. 120. MA 6304.10.28 (recto). Dummy for p. 47.

No. 121. MA 6304.9.3. Variant dummy for p. 46.

No. 122. MA 6304.5.20. Study for pp. 46–47.

No. 123. MA 6304.10.28 (verso). Dummy for p. 48.

No. 124. MA 6304.01. Maquette, p. 36 (corresponding to p. 46 of published book).

No. 125. MA 6304.9.4. Variant dummy for p. 48.

Laurent de Brunhoff's *Babar et ce coquin d'Arthur*, pp. 102–43

Detail on p. 102: Laurent de Brunhoff. *Babar et ce coquin d'Arthur*. Study for p. 43, detail. For full image, see No. 201.
MA 6305.1.37.

Laurent de Brunhoff's drawings have been arranged in the following groups.

MA 6305.1
Watercolor studies (53). Dimensions vary.

MA 6305.2
Black line drawings (27), used by the printer to generate black line proofs. Ca. 22 × 14.5 inches (56 × 37 cm); dimensions vary.

MA 6305.3
Ink and watercolor studies (4). Dimensions vary.

MA 6305.4
Finished watercolors over black line proof (26), used by the printer to produce the first edition. Double-page drawings: ca. 22 × 14.5 inches (56 × 37 cm); single-page drawings: ca. 14.5 × 11 inches (37 × 28) cm; dimensions vary.

No. 126. MA 6305.1.01. Study for cover.

No. 127. MA 6305.2.01. Black line drawing for cover.

No. 128. MA 6305.4.01. Dummy for title page.

No. 129. MA 6305.1.02 (recto). Study for p. 3.

No. 130. MA 6305.4.02. Dummy for p. 3.

No. 131. MA 6305.1.02 (verso). Study for pp. 4–5.

No. 132. MA 6305.1.03. Study for pp. 4–5.

No. 133. MA 6305.1.04. Study for pp. 4–5.

No. 134. MA 6305.1.05. Study for pp. 4–5.

No. 135. MA 6305.4.03. Dummy for pp. 4–5.

No. 136. MA 6305.1.06. Study for p. 6.

No. 137. MA 6305.1.07. Study for p. 7.

No. 138. MA 6305.1.11. Study for pp. 7 and 10.

No. 139. MA 6305.4.04a–b. Dummy for pp. 6–7.

No. 140. MA 6305.1.08. Study for p. 8.

No. 141. MA 6305.1.09. Study for p. 8.

No. 142. MA 6305.1.10 (recto). Study for p. 9.

No. 143. MA 6305.4.05a–b. Dummy for pp. 8–9.

No. 144. MA 6305.1.10 (verso). Study for p. 10.

No. 145. MA 6305.1.12 (recto). Study for p. 11.

No. 146. MA 6305.4.06a–b. Dummy for pp. 10–11.

No. 147. MA 6305.1.12 (verso). Study for pp. 12–13.

No. 148. MA 6305.4.07. Dummy for p. 12–13.

No. 149. MA 6305.1.13. Study for p. 14.

No. 150. MA 6305.1.14 (recto). Study for p. 15.
No. 151. MA 6305.4.08. Dummy for pp. 14–15.
No. 152. MA 6305.1.14 (verso). Study for p. 16.
No. 153. MA 6305.1.15. Study for p. 16.
No. 154. MA 6305.1.16. Study for p. 16.
No. 155. MA 6305.1.17. Study for p. 16.
No. 156. MA 6305.1.18. Study for p. 17.
No. 157. MA 6305.1.20 (recto). Study for p. 17.
No. 158. MA 6305.4.09a–b. Dummy for pp. 16–17.
No. 159. MA 6305.1.19. Study for pp. 18–19.
No. 160. MA 6305.1.20 (verso). Study for pp. 18–19.
No. 161. MA 6305.4.10. Dummy for pp. 18–19.
No. 162. MA 6305.1.21. Study for pp. 20–21.
No. 163. MA 6305.4.11. Dummy for pp. 20–21.
No. 164. MA 6305.1.22 (verso). Study for p. 22.
No. 165. MA 6305.1.23 (recto). Study for p. 23.
No. 166. MA 6305.1.22 (recto). Study for pp. 22–23.
No. 167. MA 6305.4.12. Dummy for pp. 22–23.
No. 168. MA 6305.1.23 (verso). Study for p. 24.
No. 169. MA 6305.1.24. Study for p. 24.
No. 170. MA 6305.1.25 (recto). Study for p. 25.
No. 171. MA 6305.4.13a–b. Dummy for pp. 24–25.
No. 172. MA 6305.1.25 (verso). Study for p. 26.
No. 173. MA 6305.1.26. Study for p. 27.
No. 174. MA 6305.1.27 (recto). Study for p. 27.
No. 175. MA 6305.4.14a–b. Dummy for pp. 26–27.
No. 176. MA 6305.1.27 (verso). Study for pp. 28–29.
No. 177. MA 6305.4.15. Dummy for pp. 28–29.
No. 178. MA 6305.1.28. Study for p. 30.
No. 179. MA 6305.4.16a–b. Dummy for pp. 30–31.
No. 180. MA 6305.3.1. Study for p. 32.
No. 181. MA 6305.3.2. Study for p. 32.

No. 182. MA 6305.3.3. Study for p. 33.
No. 183. MA 6305.1.29 (recto). Study for p. 33.
No. 184. MA 6305.4.17. Dummy for p. 32.
No. 185. MA 6305.4.18. Dummy for p. 33.
No. 186. MA 6305.1.29 (verso). Study for p. 34.
No. 187. MA 6305.1.30. Study for pp. 34–35.
No. 188. MA 6305.1.31. Study for p. 35.
No. 189. MA 6305.1.32. Study for pp. 36, 38, or cover.
No. 190. MA 6305.4.19. Dummy for pp. 34–35.
No. 191. MA 6305.4.20. Dummy for pp. 36–37.
No. 192. MA 6305.1.33. Study for p. 38.
No. 193. MA 6305.1.34. Study for p. 38.
No. 194. MA 6305.1.35 (recto). Study for p. 39.
No. 195. MA 6305.4.21a–b. Dummy for pp. 38–39.
No. 196. MA 6305.1.35 (verso). Study for p. 40.
No. 197. MA 6305.1.36 (recto). Study for p. 41.
No. 198. MA 6305.3.4. Study for pp. 40–41.
No. 199. MA 6305.4.22a–b. Dummy for pp. 40–41.
No. 200. MA 6305.1.36 (verso). Study for p. 42.
No. 201. MA 6305.1.37. Study for p. 43.
No. 202. MA 6305.4.23a–b. Dummy for pp. 42–43.
No. 203. MA 6305.1.38. Study for pp. 44–45.
No. 204. MA 6305.4.24. Dummy for pp. 44–45.
No. 205. MA 6305.1.39a. Study for p. 46.
No. 206. MA 6305.1.39b. Study for p. 47.
No. 207. MA 6305.4.25a–b. Dummy for pp. 46–47.
No. 208. MA 6305.1.39 (verso). Study for p. 48.
No. 209. MA 6305.4.26. Dummy for p. 48.

Masthead, p. 152
Laurent de Brunhoff, *Babar et ce coquin d'Arthur*.
Dummy for pp. 28–29, detail. For full image, see No. 177.

Credits

Published by The Morgan Library & Museum

Karen Banks, *Publications Manager*
Patricia Emerson, *Senior Editor*
Rose Miesner, *Editorial Assistant*

PROJECT STAFF
Christine Nelson, *Drue Heinz Curator of
Literary and Historical Manuscripts*

Marilyn Palmeri, *Photography and Rights Manager*
Eva Soos, *Photography and Rights Assistant Manager*
Alessandra Merrill, *Photography and Rights Administrative Assistant*

Robert DeCandido, *Database Coordinator*

Reba F. Snyder, *Conservator*
Denise Stockman, *Sherman Fairchild Fellow, Paper Conservation*

French language consulting by Christine Moisset

Designed by Bessas & Ackerman
Printed by Meridian Printing, East Greenwich, RI
Bound by Acme Bookbinding
Printed on PhoeniXmotion Xantur
in typefaces Electra LH and Futura